TH

NATION

OF VI

THE
NATIONAL GALLERY
OF VICTORIA

URSULA HOFF
Assistant Director

with an introduction by
ERIC WESTBROOK
Director

217 ILLUSTRATIONS, 30 IN COLOUR

THAMES AND HUDSON · LONDON

Printed in Switzerland by Rotosadag, Geneva
Bound in West Germany by Hollmann KG, Darmstadt

ISBN 0 500 18139 x cloth
ISBN 0 500 20133 1 paper

Contents

Introduction

The National Gallery of Victoria is perhaps the least known of the larger public collections. Situated in a continent still thought to be remote from Europe and the Americas, it has yet to become a staging-point on one of the international tracks trodden by museum staffs and critics. At the same time, the collections, the quality of which can be judged from the illustrations and Dr Ursula Hoff's descriptions in this book, were not derived from one royal, aristocratic or private source, but have been built up over more than a century. Only in such cases as the acquisition of the Blake watercolours from the Linnell collection, the Tiepolo *Banquet of Cleopatra* from the Hermitage and Sir Thomas Barlow's superb collection of Dürer engravings have sudden or spectacular additions drawn the attention of scholars and specialists to the institution. Yet the Gallery contains many agreeable and exciting objects which have the added interest of now being located in a country which has known European settlement for only one hundred and ninety-four years.

The credit for this achievement goes to a number of private benefactors, Governments, Trustees and professional officers who have served and supported the institution since the presentation to the public of its rather odd nucleus in 1861. Some of the more interesting and energetic personalities among these people will be noted here. First on the stage must be Redmond Barry who, like so many of his contemporaries and successors who have shaped Australia, was born (1813) in Ireland. There he was admitted to the Bar, but Ireland could not satisfy his ambitions, and he left for Australia to settle in that part of the colony of New South Wales which was to secede in 1851 and become the State of Victoria. Barry's ambitions should have been satisfied there, for he became Chief Justice of the Supreme Court, was knighted and elected first Chancellor of the University of Melbourne, Senior Trustee of the Public (now State) Library of Victoria, and was a driving force behind the foundation of the National Gallery. It is perhaps of some interest that Barry sentenced the bushranger Ned Kelly to death in

1880 and, as predicted by Kelly, almost immediately followed his victim to the grave, although by less violent means.

On 3 July 1854, Barry, having assisted at the laying of the foundation stone of Melbourne University, went on to lay another stone upon which the Library was to rise, and used the occasion to sum up his contribution by saying: 'Seventeen years have scarcely elapsed since the foundation of the colony which was then inhabited by savages. Probably in the world's history no country has attempted to found both a University and a Public Library within a score of years of its first settlement.' Five years later, extensions to the new Library building were already being discussed and in May 1859 £2,000 was voted by the Government for the purchase of works of art to form the basis of a public collection.

At that time, purchase meant almost inevitably purchase in England, and therefore the Trustees headed by Barry asked two of their colleagues who had returned there to carry out a policy of buying laid down in Melbourne. This policy now sounds alarming, if not positively perverse, in the light of the material which was available in Europe in the 1860s. It demanded that the purchase of original paintings and sculpture should be avoided and that attention should be concentrated on photographs of works of art, casts, coins, gems and, rather charmingly, 'objects of miscellaneous vertue'. Barry's hand can be seen in this, and he was probably motivated by a desire to plant a sound classical taste in a raw young civilization. Most of the objects first acquired cannot now be traced, and in fact all were nearly lost in transit, finally being landed in Melbourne so badly damaged by sea-water that Barry wrote: 'Our Museum looks at present like a field of battle, such is the mutilation.' But first-aid treatment was applied quickly enough for the Governor, Sir Henry Barkly, to open the Museum of Art (as it was first called) in the Library building on 24 May 1861. Within two months, it had been visited by 62,000 curious and culture-starved colonists. These people found themselves among 'casts of the Elgin Marbles, seventy antique statues (also casts), sixty-three busts and a quantity of other art objects'. Clearly, these visitors were proud of their collection, whatever its limitations, as citizens of Victoria have remained of the Gallery into which it has grown.

It is appropriate here to note the apparent contradiction whereby a State institution bears the title of 'National Gallery'. The Gallery in Melbourne was the first of those which were founded in each of the capital cities of the Australian States during the nineteenth century. Their proud begetters saw them as the direct offspring of the National Gallery in London, and each at first bore the same title to signify a collection of works of art open to the public and sustained by public funds; today, only Victoria retains this usage.

In the year of the opening of the gallery of casts, an English migrant artist, Thomas Clark, who had been head of schools of art and design in Nottingham and Birmingham, proposed to the State Government that a School of Art should be founded in direct association with the collection. The idea was well received; the National Gallery School of Art became part of the institution, and was indeed at first such a dominant part that the main duties of the Director were as head teacher in the School. As the collections grew, the balance changed and later the Head of the School was an artist working under the administrative responsibility of the Director of the Gallery. The School has had a proud record and has produced many of Australia's most distinguished artists. With all this activity, the Government saw the need to lay down future policies for the growth and use of the collections, and in October 1863, a Commission on the Fine Arts was set up with eleven members and with Barry as its Chairman. This body set to work in 1864, and at its first meeting Barry announced that the Government had put £1,000 at its disposal for the purchase of paintings.

From that moment the Gallery became a battleground, not of damaged casts but of conflicting opinions. This tradition still continues and has been on the whole healthy, although there have been losses both of desirable works which should have been acquired and of admirable advisers who have retired hurt.

But at first there was general agreement that Sir Charles Eastlake, a painter who was President of the Royal Academy, Director of the London National Gallery and an authority on the methods and materials of painting, should be asked to 'designate a certain number of original paintings by modern artists which in his opinion [were] suitable to be placed in the Victorian Gallery of Art'. Eastlake was told by Barry that the Gallery would have a teaching function, and that the Commissioners were already divided on the desirability of acquiring original works or copies of great masterpieces. In the 1860s in England, popular painting was experiencing a boom, and, therefore, the £1,000 (whether the Commissioners knew it or not) would not have gone far either way. It went, in fact, into such works as *A Fern Gatherer* by R. Herdman, *Sheep in Repose* by E. Tschaggeny and *Le Départ du fiancé* by G. Koller, the only artist of any consequence on the list being J. F. Herring, who was represented by one of his farmyard pieces. One other interesting name was that of G. F. Folingsby, who was later to become

9

the first Director of the Gallery. These works, unlike the casts, still exist, and therefore one can reflect on the way in which the colonists' money was spent. Without doubt, fine Italian, Flemish and German primitives, with which Eastlake was familiar, could have been acquired at reasonable prices, and on this account he may be held guilty of condescension to and betrayal of the young Gallery. On the other hand, it is extremely doubtful if those who controlled the Gallery and the Government purse in Melbourne would have understood such works or thanked him for suggesting them. In this first group, a number of Australian paintings were also bought, and the seeds were sown of a long and continuing argument as to which Australian artists should be supported and to what extent.

In 1865 the Government of Victoria accepted the final report of the Commission on the Fine Arts, and its work ended. This report recommended, among other things, that whilst original pictures should form the basis and chief part of the National Collection, a limited number of copies of pictures in European national collections should be obtained. It also said 'that the selection of pictures in future should proceed upon an organized system . . . so as to illustrate history, both sacred and secular, poetry, domestic life, landscape, portraiture, and those subjects more immediately required for instruction in drawing'. Perhaps most important of all, it urged 'that a suitable gallery should be built upon the [land] set apart by the Government for the Public Library and the Museum'.

Popular anecdotal paintings continued to enter the collection, and the first picture gallery to house them was opened on 1 December 1864. But the tide began to turn with the appointment in 1891 of a new Director who was to remain in office for over forty years. Bernard Hall was thirty-three when he arrived in Melbourne. He had studied painting in London, Antwerp and Munich, and was a founder member of the New English Art Club. Hall was to be responsible for many changes in the Gallery, and even his first purchases, conservative as they were – they included a flower piece by Fantin-Latour and two drawings by Du Maurier – showed a freshness of approach. From this time a new professionalism appeared, for Hall was conscientious in his duties, prepared reports which expressed his views to the Trustees with force and clarity, and showed remarkable perception in many of his recommendations for additions to the collection. But he was so sure of his taste that he became stubborn and resentful of outside opinion. This tendency unfortunately increased as he grew older, although it had one valuable result in his last years.

The value of Hall's appointment increased when in 1904 a wealthy Melbourne merchant, Alfred Felton, died leaving a large estate in trust with provision for hospitals and charities and an equal amount for the National Gallery of Victoria. It was upon the basis of the Felton Bequest that the present fortunes of the Gallery were founded. Hall immediately saw the possibility of building up a collection of quality, and in an urgent report quoted the novelist George Moore: 'the original taste of man is always for the obvious and the commonplace and . . . it is only by great labour and care that man learns to understand as beautiful that which the uneducated eye considers ugly'. But there were problems, one of which was that Alfred Felton stated that a European adviser should be employed to recommend suitable works. Many of these advisers were to find Hall, the Trustees and the Committee which handled the Felton Bequest difficult to work with, but Hall got in first by proposing that he should go to Europe to make the first purchases under the terms of the Bequest. This was approved by the bodies involved, and he arrived in Europe in February 1905. The achievements of this journey are still major objects in the collections, and include the magnificent Pissarro *Boulevard Montmartre*, a carving and a bronze by Rodin, and Turner's *Oakhampton*. Hall wrote to Melbourne that he would have liked to buy a Monet, a Sisley and a Degas from the Impressionist Exhibition from which the Pissarro came, but that the prices were prohibitive. He had paid £300 for the Pissarro.

On Hall's return to Australia, the same battles raged, and only the quality of the combatants varied. The Felton Adviser in London in 1909 was a certain Frank Gibson, who was permitted to call in specialists including Roger Fry, Charles Ricketts and Percy Macquoid for special advice. But the acquisitions which resulted were hardly of the quality which such distinguished names might suggest. Hall was more positive. He wrote: 'I have brooded over this question of Gallery standards for nearly twenty years, apart from my practice as an artist, and am as well able to give an opinion in these things as another. For this reason I could, I think, had I the opportunity, explain to the Trustees why, out of the score of works in the last batch, so few are satisfactory, and why it appears to me a poor result for so vast an expenditure.'

This threw the challenge back, and various expedients were tried, including broader areas of consultation; under this provision, Sir Sidney Colvin entered the field as an additional Felton Adviser. But when Colvin and Gibson recommended what they considered major works, these had to run the gauntlet of Hall, the Trustees and the Felton Bequest Committee and were often rejected. The rejections included two Gainsboroughs, the *Portrait of Lord Hampden* and one of his 'fancy pictures'. On 2 March 1915 Colvin, oppressed by an art war on top of the real conflict, offered his resignation, and in 1917 Robert Ross was appointed Adviser. This was in the climate of both British and Australian opinion an enlightened but extraordinary choice. 'Robbie' Ross had been Oscar Wilde's most loyal friend, his literary executor and his biographer. After his death, his ashes were placed in Wilde's tomb in the cemetery of Père-Lachaise in Paris. He held the position of Felton Adviser for only a year before he died, and he was never able to make the journey to Melbourne which he looked forward to, but he bought two beautiful Pre-Raphaelite paintings, *The Garden of Pan* by Burne-Jones and *La Belle Dame sans Merci* by Arthur Hughes, as well as others of less interest. His greatest achievement was to penetrate the three lines of defence in Melbourne with thirty-six watercolours from Blake's series of illustrations to Dante's *Divine Comedy*, together with other drawings and engravings by the same artist. Not that the defenders surrendered tamely: one Trustee who saw the works in London, clearly puzzled and disturbed, described them as 'quaint', surely the first and last time this adjective has been applied to William Blake.

With these works, the Felton Bequest Committee seems to have realized its potential power to buy in the international market. The next Adviser was perhaps not so widely known as Ross, but Frank Rinder performed his duties magnificently. His advice was stimulating, sane and realistic, and the purchases reflected these qualities. They included the great Van Dyck *The Countess of Southampton*, *Walton Bridges* by Turner, the exquisite *Wharncliffe Book of Hours*, Memling's *Man of Sorrows in the Arms of the Virgin*, the Titian *Portrait of a Monk* and the Ince-Blundell *Madonna and Child*, now no longer attributed to Van Eyck, but still a magical and much admired work. At the same time, many objects which should now grace the collections were declined; and in 1926, with uninformed local criticisms and pressures mounting, Rinder resigned, to be replaced by Randall Davies, to whom we owe the recommendation of the Rembrandt *Self-portrait* from Welbeck Abbey and the great Tiepolo *Banquet of Cleopatra* from the Hermitage. Davies' appointment was not renewed when the agreement expired in 1934, and a new policy was adopted whereby an adviser was to be sent from Australia, with the advantage of knowing the Melbourne collections intimately, and therefore able to recommend on a surer basis.

The only possible person to launch such a policy was the Director, Bernard Hall, who was now seventy-three, and he left for London in February 1934 to take up the post which he had long wished for and which he felt he could best fill. But even now under what must have seemed to Hall the most ideal conditions, there was trouble. Sir Charles Holmes, painter and Director of the National Gallery in London, had been frequently consulted in the past (he jointly recommended the Tiepolo with Davies), and he and Hall had failed to agree. Now they were to work together, and Hall was expected by his Committee in Melbourne to consult Holmes on possible Felton purchases. This he refused to do, and matters came to a head over Hall's enthusiastic recommendation of the early Rembrandt *The Two Philosophers*. The battle was long and complicated, but eventually the painting was acquired and, to quote Dr Leonard Cox (*The National Gallery of Victoria 1861-1968. A search for a collection*, N.G.V., 1970), 'It may be regarded as a monument to Bernard Hall and as perhaps his greatest recommendation'. Bernard Hall died in London in 1935. He had made his mark in many ways, as a teacher, as an honest if not remarkable painter, but most of all, despite the handicap of an almost obsessional belief in his own powers, as a great Director – great if only for *Boulevard Montmartre*, bought on his first official visit to London, and *The Two Philosophers*, bought on his last.

Now the Gallery needed a new Director and the Felton Bequest Committee a new Adviser. The first post was filled by James MacDonald, previously Director of the Sydney Gallery, and the second by Sir Sydney Cockerell. The names were different, but again the battle was the same, in that MacDonald refused to countenance any work of the 'modern' school (by which he meant Cézanne and Van Gogh) which even the conservative Cockerell might suggest. That good works by both artists were acquired seems more by good fortune than by good will. At this point one can happily turn to the more positive and indeed exciting developments which began at about the beginning of the Second World War.

In 1945 the Trust which had conducted the affairs of the Library, two Science Museums and the National Gallery was split into separate bodies and Sir Keith Murdoch, a newspaper proprietor and a powerful figure in Australian life, became Chairman of the National Gallery Trustees. Already in 1941 Daryl (now Sir Daryl) Lindsay, a painter and a member of a famous family of artists, had succeeded MacDonald as Director, and he and Murdoch worked closely together. Fresh advice now came from John

13

Gian Battista Tiepolo *The Banquet of Cleopatra* 1743–44 (see p. 42)

McDonnell and Sir Kenneth (now Lord) Clark in London, who acted jointly for the Felton Bequest. These men served the Gallery so well that from this time policies began to be based on perception rather than prejudice. At the same time, the results of three major benefactions made themselves felt: that of Mr H. W. Kent, consisting of superb Chinese ceramics and bronzes which formed the basis of an important Department; the large Howard Spensley Bequest of paintings, drawings and sculpture which included a remarkable Bassano portrait and a Rodin bronze, and the gift from Mrs Colin Templeton of a wide range of English porcelain which changed the face of this area of the Gallery. From Felton resources came a fine Florentine profile portrait and a third Rembrandt, *Portrait of an Unknown Man*. At the same time, consideration was given to the present and future housing of the collections.

In 1943 Dr Ursula Hoff, a specialist in Rembrandt studies, who is now Assistant Director, joined the staff as Assistant Keeper of Prints and Drawings, and soon the Print Room and its display area had been completely

Anthony van Dyck *The·Countess of Southampton* c. 1640 (see p. 35) ►

Rachel 1ˢᵗ Countess of
Southampton.

redesigned and renovated. But no changes to the old building, however drastic, could make it suitable for all the purposes of a modern gallery, and a new building was clearly essential.

Fortunately, help was at hand. In 1943 there was already throughout Australia a sense of the need for post-war planning. The Trustees of the Library were not to be left out of this general surge of activity, and architects were commissioned to report on the future development of the various institutions. Their recommendation was that the National Gallery of Victoria should be housed in a new building sited on Crown land in St Kilda Road, a broad boulevard leading straight into the main areas of the city of Melbourne. Armed with this report, the Trustees led by Sir Keith Murdoch called upon the Government for action, and from that time until his death in 1950 Sir Keith was a staunch, constant and active supporter of the proposal. At the same time, stirred by the prospect of the St Kilda Road site becoming available, a group of people, including the distinguished composer Dr Margaret Sutherland, set up the Combined Arts Centre Movement to urge that suitable accommodation for the performing arts should be found on the same site. The Government was sympathetic, but it was not until 1955, when the Government of Mr (now Sir Henry) Bolte took office, that action was taken.

In 1956 the present writer succeeded Sir Daryl Lindsay as Director, and within a short time of taking office was asked by the party in power for a report on the nature and components of an Arts Centre to serve all the arts. This report was then used as a basis for legislation enabling the project to go ahead, with the National Gallery given priority in the building programme. The next twelve years were full of incident and progress. A further and extended brief from the Director and his staff was used as the basis for the programme given to the chosen architect, Mr (now Sir Roy) Grounds. While the staff and the architect's team worked closely together, over $1,200,000 was raised from donors in large and small sums, all of which bore testimony to the same enthusiasm for the Gallery that had been evident in 1861, exactly one hundred years earlier.

As the building went ahead, changes were occurring in the collections and the staff. In 1956 came the acquisition by the Felton Bequest Committee of the great collection of Dürer engravings (including books) which had been brought together over many years by the English industrialist Sir Thomas Barlow. This gave the already important Department of Prints and Drawings a further dimension. The bequest of Mr Everard Studley Miller in the same year brought a large sum of money and several valuable properties to the Gallery on condition that the funds should be used for the acquisition of 'portraits of persons of merit in history . . . before 1800'. A remarkable number of fine paintings, sculptures and prints have been acquired from the Miller Bequest, including the great bust of Richelieu by Bernini and the engravings of the series known as the *Iconography* by Van Dyck. From Felton sources came such important objects as the last available cast of the *Balzac* by Rodin. On the death of John McDonnell in 1964 Dr Mary Woodall was appointed Felton Adviser.

The new building was opened on 20 August 1968, to general approval and many professional congratulations. It had been designed to accommodate a greatly increased staff, now grouped in seven curatorial departments and a Department of Exhibitions and Display with subdivisions for Glass, Ceramics, Metalwork, Furniture and Textiles coming under the general heading of Decorative Arts. More recently a Department of Photography, the first in Australia, has been added and is now in full operation.

In the first four years in the new building, over four million people visited the National Gallery, and, with the generous space available for exhibitions, it can be confidently expected that this level of attendance will continue. This success has led to further generous donations, among the most important of which is the William and Margaret Morgan Endowment for the acquisition of domestic glass, which has already purchased the fine Gordon Russell collection for the Gallery. It would seem that the Gallery is again in one of its great periods of development, and the grant of direct funds from the State Government which led to the purchase of the great Carracci study of a nude for the Palazzo Farnese decorations (formerly in the Ellesmere Collection) points to new sources of finance and development.

This book will show that there are many areas of collection still to be developed; but it will also show that within one hundred and ten years a strong overall collection has been created, and properly housed, and that the Gallery has had much support and encouragement from the community which it serves. We are now happy, through this book, to introduce this collection to a wider audience.

ERIC WESTBROOK
Director

EUROPEAN AND AMERICAN PAINTING AND SCULPTURE

FLORENTINE SCHOOL (15th century)   Italian
The Adoration of the Magi, 1420–30
Tempera on wood, $7\frac{1}{8} \times 18\frac{1}{2}$ in (18.1 × 47 cm)

In his book *On Painting*, Leon Battista Alberti said: 'An admirable and praiseworthy narrative picture will present itself so charming and adorned with pleasant features that it will hold anyone who looks at it, taught or untaught, in delight and emotion.' Spectators never cease to delight in the order and variety of the *Adoration*. The bustle of overlapping forms of horses and camels on the left is followed by the separate, distinctly silhouetted figures of the Three Kings and Joseph; the eye travels over the prostrate body of the old King towards the goal of their journey and the close of the composition: the Virgin, framed by the cloth of honour and the shed, is distanced from the rest of the scene by the white and shaded walls of the building on her left. The ordered design, to which the undulating hillside plays an accompaniment, is that of the early Renaissance. Variety is added by the splendour of the costumes and the brilliant colours, which still echo the gay fairytale style of courtly Gothic. The elongated format suggests that the picture once formed part of the predella of a large altarpiece.

The work has belonged to Professor Sellars of Edinburgh, Archibald Anderson, Archibald George Blomefield Russell, Herbert Bier, London, The Schaeffer Galleries, New York, and Herbert Bier, London, from whom it was acquired in 1966–67 under the terms of the Felton Bequest.

FLORENTINE SCHOOL (15th century)   Italian
Profile Portrait of a Lady, 1450–75
Tempera or oil on panel, 17 × 11 ⅝ in (43.2 × 29.5 cm)

The small picture has the brilliance of a many-faceted jewel. The horns of
the Burgundian headdress give an exotic, mask-like quality to the elaborate
silhouette of the head. The meticulously outlined profile shares precision of
form with the elaborate pieces of jewellery which adorn the richly brocaded
dress and the headband. The portrait is part of a group of Florentine profile
portraits dating from the middle of the fifteenth century, some of which
have been attributed to the goldsmith, sculptor and painter Antonio
Pollaiuolo. They certainly suggest an affinity with the fine chiselling of a
goldsmith. The light-toned head, set against a dark ground which blends
with the tone of the dress, has a cameo-like prominence. The profile portrait
of the Renaissance, inspired by the heads on the coins and gems of classical
antiquity, testifies to a new interest in the individual personality.

    The picture was in the possession of Alexander Barker, from whence it
came into the Cook Collection in Richmond; it was acquired from there in
1946 under the terms of the Felton Bequest.

UNKNOWN SCULPTOR (15th century)   French
St Barbara, 1420–30

Oak, h. 43 in (109.2 cm)

Dating from the end of the Middle Ages, the insubstantial figure swings in
the late Gothic stance. The folds of the garment, made from heavy, perhaps
woollen materials, are the Gothic carver's chief means of expression. The
material creates its own life; the billows and crevices accumulate in fine,
rectilinear motifs along the sleeve, as if suggesting the mobility of the arm.
The triangular, sharply undercut, edgy forms of the mantle play a counter-
point to the fine, soft, parallel folds of the dress. Fold masses cascade down
on the left in response to the gathering up of the mantle by the hand, and
amplify the silhouette of the figure, balancing the slightly inward-leaning
tower on the other side. The alliance of simplicity and richness in the fold

motifs echoes the union of Christian devotion and aristocratic elegance in the saint.

According to the *Golden Legend*, St Barbara was immured in a tower by her father who was opposed to her marriage; she was beheaded by him when she adopted the Christian faith. The statue was originally poly-chromed, but seems to have been deliberately stripped of paint in the nineteenth century.

It was acquired in New York under the terms of the Felton Bequest in 1946.

HANS MEMLING (active 1466, died 1494)   Flemish
The Man of Sorrows in the Arms of the Virgin, 1475
Oil on panel, $16^{13}/_{16} \times 7^{7}/_{8}$ in (27.4 × 19.9 cm)

Christ bearing the wounds of the Crucifixion, yet upright and alive, is a visionary image known as the 'Gregorian Man of Sorrows', since it is said to have appeared to Pope Gregory during the celebration of a mass. Memling's Virgin is the 'Mater Dolorosa' whose tears flow for the suffering of her Son. This imagery was widely popular in the late fifteenth century and had been the subject of an altarpiece by Memling's master, Rogier van der Weyden, as we know from an inventory of the art collection of Margaret of Austria, Regent of the Netherlands. 'When it came to the expression of sorrowful compassion, the memory of Rogier came to [Memling's] aid,' wrote Max Friedlander. We do not know how closely Memling followed his prototype, but Rogier excelled in the representation of 'bitter-sweet sorrow', and sometimes placed his sacred figures on the medieval gold ground which Memling uses here. It gives a dream-like quality to the minutely realized faces and figures, which summarize the story of the Passion and seem to float in a spaceless *ambiente* of light.

A lesser master than Rogier, Memling appears to greatest advantage in small works. His miniature-fine execution lies above a surprisingly impul-sive underdrawing. We can see with the naked eye, and even better with infra-red photographs, lines drawn with a fine brush and neutral tint on the white gesso ground, with which, by trial and error, the final disposition of shapes has been arrived at. Memling overlaid his underdrawing with pig-ment, but this has become transparent with age and some of the drawing reappears, such as that of the arms and hands of Christ.

Some time before 1900, the picture had come into the possession of a second-hand dealer in Caen, from whom it was purchased between 1900 and 1905 by Théodore Griveau of Connerré (Sarthe). After the 1914–18 war it appeared on the art market and was acquired in London in 1924 under the terms of the Felton Bequest.

REMBRANDT VAN RIJN (1606-1669)   Dutch
The Two Philosophers, 1628
Oil on panel, $28^7/_8 \times 23^1/_2$ in (73.4 × 59.7 cm)

'The greatest rebel in the history of painting': so a contemporary critic
referred to Rembrandt. The rebellion the writer had in mind was Rembrandt's rejection of the classical tradition of idealized youth and physical
intactness. He introduced an unprecedented range of observations from life
into his work, among them the infirmity of body and ardour of spirit of the
very old, and the effect of run-down, ramshackle architecture, elevated into
poetry by light and shade. From his youth Rembrandt adopted the dramatic light-dark effects which had been brought to Utrecht by the Dutch

followers of Caravaggio, and which here fill the cell-like room and cast a glow over the disputing figures. The subject remains obscure; the spirit of it is conveyed in a poem by the English seventeenth-century poet John Elsum:

> Conscience has made the Hoary Father nice,
> He quits the World to fly from Noise and Vice,
> Renounces all its Honours, Pleasures, Riches
> And every Vanity that Man bewitches.
> His garments coarse, his Diet very slender,
> His Body worn with age, and very tender. . . .
>
> For placing his delight in Contemplation
> He in a Cell enjoys the whole Creation.

The picture first belonged to Jacob de Gheyn III, who died in 1644, then to Joannes Wytenbogaert. In 1743 it was in the collection of Signor Bartolo Bernardi of San Apollinare, but its later history is unknown. It was acquired in 1934 in Amsterdam under the terms of the Felton Bequest.

After JAN VAN EYCK (c. 1390–1441)   Flemish
The Virgin and Child
Oil on panel, $10^3/_8 \times 7^5/_8$ in (26.4 × 19.5 cm)

Contemplating an illuminated manuscript, the Virgin and Child are seated in a homely room filled with furniture and objects of medieval Flemish daily use, which contrast curiously with the large figures and the brocaded baldachin. Jan van Eyck's greatest achievement lay in his control of light effects and in the use of normal perspective, which, for the first time in European art, gave his rooms a natural look. He employed naturalism to create effects of splendour reminiscent of the bejewelled consecrated objects of the medieval Church, and combined this effect with the conviction that a religious work must teach; the objects and figures contain a hidden sermon. Behind Mary, the Queen of Heaven, rises a regal baldachin, but she wears no crown and sits low on the ground; she is both humble and exalted. The candlestick carries a candle as the Virgin carries the Child; its earthly light has been superseded by the heavenly light which fills the room. The light passes through a glass carafe, an allusion to the Virginity of the divine mother; the apples on the window-sill recall the Fall and remind the believer that Mary is the new Eve and Christ the Redeemer.

The picture was discovered by the German art historian Waagen in the chaplain's room at Ince Hall in 1850, and subsequently figured in literature as an original Van Eyck until in 1957 and 1958 it was examined at the Institut Royal du Patrimoine Artistique in Brussels, when it was found that the paint constituents and the structure of the paint layers were inconsistent with fifteenth-century Flemish practice. It was acquired from Ince Hall in 1921 under the terms of the Felton Bequest.

SIMON MARMION (active 1449, died 1489)   French–Flemish
The Virgin and Child, 1465–75
Oil on panel, 15 × 11 in (38.1 × 28 cm)

Less jewel-like than the Eyckian Madonna, Marmion's picture is also less mysterious; its message is easily read. The Virgin is withdrawn in prayer and seems haunted by foreknowledge of the Child's fate. Enacting his future role as Teacher and Saviour, Jesus blesses the worshipper. The half-figure of Virgin and Child had been unusual in northern painting until the time of Rogier van der Weyden, who introduced the motif in 1450 on his return from a visit to Italy, where it was popular as a devotional image. Simon Marmion closely followed Rogier's style; if his outline is less sharp, his technique of painting has the finesse for which the Flemish school has become famous. His panel is covered with buff-coloured gesso. The design has been carried out in coloured glazes which in the lighter parts have developed a fine network of cracks. The colour scheme, in which blues, blue greys and light browns predominate, well supports the mood of sorrow inherent in Marmion's theme.

The painting was in the Czartorisky collection in Cracow and Paris until 1939; it was acquired in 1954 under the terms of the Felton Bequest.

WORKSHOP OF PIETER VAN DER WEYDEN (1437–1514) Flemish
Triptych with the Miracles of Christ (left wing)
Oil on panel, $44^1/_2 \times 14^3/_8$ in (113×37.2 cm)

Towards the end of the fifteenth century the lesser Flemish painters, those
who could not free themselves from the burden of the great tradition to
which they were the heirs, tended to combine features from various schools.

The Marriage at Cana belongs to a triptych which is executed in the tradition of Rogier van der Weyden. The wing here combines Rogierian traits with those of Dirk Bouts, whose *Last Supper* in Louvain has inspired many of the features of this scene; but the choice of subject is singular in Flemish fifteenth-century painting. *The Marriage*, set in a Flemish banqueting-hall, takes place in the presence of several generations of the House of Burgundy; starting at the far end of the long arm of the table we see Philip the Good of Burgundy, Margaret of York and her husband Charles the Bold of Burgundy, followed by Mary of Burgundy and her husband, Emperor Maximilian I of Hapsburg, and their son Philip the Fair. In the foreground, Engelbert of Nassau acts as cup-bearer to the governor of the feast, Adolph of Cleves. Most of the heads are close to still-existing portraits by Rogier van der Weyden and other painters. The choice of so many individualized faces, and the colourful variety of the costumes, may be inspired by the characteristically Flemish concern with minute particulars. Any other reason for the inclusion of these portraits remains obscure.

The triptych was in the Gsell collection in Vienna. It was acquired in 1922 under the terms of the Felton Bequest from Lady Leyland, London.

TITIAN (active before 1511, died 1576)   Italian
Bust of a Franciscan Friar with a Book, c. 1550
Oil on canvas, $33^{1}/_{4} \times 29^{3}/_{8}$ in (84.5 × 74.6 cm)

Compared with the *Profile Portrait of a Lady* of about forty years earlier, Titian's portrait exemplifies the change that had come over Italian culture in the intervening years. Dignity and simplicity are now the keynotes. The vitality of the life-size, frontally-seen sitter is conveyed by glance and attitude. The body, clad in uniform black, acts simply as a base for the head, which carries the strongest light.

The sense of conscious greatness which emanates from this portrait is new in European art. Titian's princely status as an artist is indirectly reflected in his dignified conception of his sitters. The handling consists of that effortless realism which calls up an illusion rather than giving a detailed description; the brushstrokes are visible in the face and partly leave the underpaint free to contribute to the shadows. How much Titian's style affected later centuries can be seen by a glance at Rembrandt's *Portrait of a Man*.

Owned by Professor Publio Podio, the portrait was acquired from Messrs Agnew of London in 1924 under the terms of the Felton Bequest.

29

Antonis Mor (1519–75)   Netherlandish
Portrait of a Lady, c. 1550–75
Oil on panel, 39½ × 28½ in (100.3 × 72.4 cm)

The sitter has not been identified. The costume, with its puffed-out shoul-
ders and long waist, as well as the lacework of the cap, suggests that the lady
is Flemish. This is a reasonable assumption, since Mor was court painter of
the Spanish Netherlands. With remarkable skill the painter has differenti-
ated between the silk and velvet, both black, and enlivened the sombre
effect by dwelling on the crimson undersleeves, the gold of buttons and
chain. Conforming to Netherlands practice, Mor always employed a high
finish, which obliterates all brushmarks, but he applied this northern method of painting to the grand, life-size, three-quarter-length portrait design he
derived from Titian.

    The painting was handed down in the younger branch of the Beckford
family, who sold it in 1875. Later owned by Mrs H. Kirby, it was acquired
under the terms of the Felton Bequest in 1948.

REMBRANDT VAN RIJN (1606–1669)   Dutch
Portrait of a Man, 1667
Oil on canvas, 43 × 36¾ in (109.2 × 93.3 cm)

This is the last commissioned portrait the artist is known to have painted. The life-size image is cut at the knees. Darkening of the colours now largely hides the wide-brimmed hat which the sitter is holding under his left hand. In a manner similar to Titian, the black, flat mass of the figure forms a base over which rises the brilliantly illuminated head. But the stability of Titian's figure has been exchanged for an asymmetrical arrangement which creates the impression of impending movement; this, together with the open brushwork of the unidealized head, demands our concentration with an intensity not required by the smooth manner practised by the more fashionable Dutch portraitists. Though Rembrandt received far fewer commissions in his last years than formerly, this picture, together with the *Syndics* of 1662, the portraits of Margareta de Geer and Jacob Trip in London and the Widener portraits in Washington, proves that the master was not forgotten.

The portrait was in the collection of the fifth Earl of Aylesford before 1836. Later owned by Alfred Beit, it was acquired in 1951 in London under the terms of the Felton Bequest.

GIAN LORENZO BERNINI (1598–1680)   Italian
The Countess Matilda, 1633–37
Bronze statuette, gilded, h. 16 in (40.5 cm)

The small figure is a cast from the original terracotta maquette modelled by
Bernini in preparation for his over life-size statue of Countess Matilda of
Tuscany, which now stands on her tomb in St Peter's in Rome. Bernini has
represented the Countess, who in her lifetime in the eleventh century had
been a great benefactress to the Holy See, as the personification of the
Papacy. In her left hand she holds the keys of St Peter, with the papal tiara
nestling in the crook of her arm; the extended right wields the sceptre of
temporal power.

While the over life-size statue in St Peter's has a large head with classical,
Junoesque features, sitting on a full columnar neck, Bernini's original
conception favoured an attenuated figure with tiny head on a delicately
modelled neck, carried out with the artifice of an earlier period and reminding us that Bernini's father was a sculptor of the era of Mannerism.

The gilded statue stands on a contemporary black marble pedestal.
According to tradition the statuette was in the collection of Prince Altieri,
later in that of Prince Ruspoli, in Rome, and then in a private collection in
Paris. It was acquired in London under the terms of the Felton Bequest in
1968–69.

GIAN LORENZO BERNINI (1598–1680)   Italian
Cardinal Richelieu
Bronze bust, h. 28¼ in (71.8 cm)

Bernini created a new conception in bust sculpture, which did not come to him suddenly but developed in stages during his life. The bronze bust of the Cardinal, cast from a life-size terracotta, slightly precedes the marble bust now in the Louvre. In the bronze, the flowing oval shape of the dress is still relatively traditional; in the marble, it is given a wavy contour suggesting a backward and forward movement of the arms which increases the effect of life and immediacy. Bernini mostly prepared his portraits by drawings. Here, however, he had to adopt a much rarer procedure; instead of being able to study the sitter in Rome, he had to use a triple portrait which Philippe de Champaigne had painted of the Cardinal in Paris.

Bernini, increasingly concerned with investing his busts with individuality and animation, greatly surpasses Champaigne in dramatic effect. Raised high above the sloping shoulder line, the head towers commandingly; the highly polished face reflects the light so that the tactile surface of the features remains tantalizingly in doubt; framed by the buoyant modelling of the hair, an intensely human person, at a specific moment in time, confronts us.

The previous history of the bronze is unknown. It was acquired in London in 1969 under the terms of the Everard Studley Miller Bequest.

NICOLAS POUSSIN (1594–1665)   French
The Crossing of the Red Sea, c. 1635
Oil on canvas, 60⅝ × 82⅝ in (154 × 209.8 cm)

A major example of 'history' painting, as the term was understood in the
seventeenth and eighteenth centuries, this work is the result of elaborate
thinking and re-thinking of the composition. The preliminary drawings are
now in the possession of the Hermitage in Leningrad. Its complex yet clear
and harmonious effect was aptly described by Poussin's first biographer,
Bellori, as 'abundant and exact'.

   The dark cloud which had led the Israelites to safety, and the Egyptians to
disaster, is straddling the sky like a storm receding after sunset. In the
foreground a group of men, one of which is posed in the attitude of Myron's
discus-thrower, salvage Egyptian armour from the sea. This combination of
close observation of nature and scholarly use of classical antique sculpture is
one of the factors which provide the 'abundance and exactness' praised by
Bellori in Poussin's work. In even rows of great complexity, Poussin shows

34

us the salvaging action of the Israelites, their thanksgiving to the Lord and, in the distance, Miriam leading the women 'with timbrels and with dances' in a song of praise.

This work and its companion piece, *The Adoration of the Golden Calf*, were painted for Amedeo del Pozzo before 1640. Having passed through various recorded ownerships, the picture was acquired from the Earl of Radnor in London in 1948 under the terms of the Felton Bequest.

ANTHONY VAN DYCK (1599–1641)   Flemish
The Countess of Southampton, c. 1640 (see p. 15)
Oil on canvas, 86 × 50½ in (118.4 × 128.2 cm)

We have a near-contemporary description of this picture by the Italian writer Bellori. 'The Countess of Southampton', he wrote, 'had been painted in the shape of the Goddess Fortune seated on a globe of the earth'. Bellori may have heard this description from Van Dyck's patron Sir Kenelm Digby. As is easily seen, he was mistaken; the Countess does not sit or stand on the globe, as figures of Fortune should, and the globe is not a terrestrial one but a crystal globe. In the emblematic language of the seventeenth century a crystal globe stands for brittle fortune. Enthroned on clouds, through which break rays of light, a death's-head under her foot and confidently leaning on the crystal globe, the Countess surely celebrates a triumph – a triumph over death and the vagaries of fortune. Van Dyck's imagery suggests that the composition was conceived posthumously: Rachel de Ruvigny, Countess of Southampton, died in February 1640. The portrait does not carry a date, but its manner of execution, as well as the costume worn by the Countess, are not incompatible with such a late date.

The portrait remained in the family of the Earls of Southampton until 1683 when it was sold to Anthony Grey, Earl of Kent, from whose descendants it passed to Lady Lucas. It was acquired from her in 1922 under the terms of the Felton Bequest.

ANTHONY VAN DYCK (1599–1641)   Flemish
Philip Herbert, Earl of Pembroke, 1635–38
Oil on canvas, 41½ × 32¾ in (105.4 × 83.2 cm)

The sharply-formed, fair, aristocratic features of the sitter rise amid a colour

chord of golden yellow, glittering black, silver white and pale blue. The colours are given added subtlety by the thin, translucent handling of the blue.

The Earl of Pembroke was Lord Chamberlain to the Royal Household of Charles I. As the owner of Wilton House he patronized the finest artists of his time; the Double Cube Room at Wilton, built by Inigo Jones, is still filled with portraits by Van Dyck.

Perhaps, as Fromentin has suggested, Van Dyck gave the people who sat to him 'something of the grace of his own person – an appearance more habitually noble, a more gallant deshabillé, a more elegant draping of garments, hands generally more beautiful, purer and whiter than they really were'; what is certain is that he has created an undying image of the brilliant court of Charles I.

The portrait came from Kyre Park in Worcestershire. In 1934 it belonged to Garabed Bishirgan. It was acquired from Colnaghi's, London, in 1937 under the terms of the Felton Bequest.

MATIA PRETI (1613–1699)   Italian
Sophonisba Receiving the Poison
Oil on canvas, 56¼ × 102 in (142.9 × 259 cm)

Heroic women stoically accepting death were a very popular theme in the seventeenth century. Preti made several versions of the moment in which the Roman general Masinissa handed a beaker of poison to the beautiful

Queen of Carthage to spare her the humiliation of marching as a prisoner in a triumphal procession through Rome. The appeal of Preti's work lies in his combination of the rich, light-dark effects of Caravaggio with the glistening armour, the Negro pages, the picturesque garments, the open verandah setting, the gold and silver tones we know from the paintings of Veronese. The broad, dry paint, scumbled over a coarse canvas, gives a decorative fresco-like texture to the scene, and assists the monumental effect of the over life-size figures.

According to tradition, the picture came from the collection of the Principi Antici Mattei, Rome, and of the Conti Gaetani, Rome. It was acquired in London in 1968 under the terms of the Felton Bequest.

SALOMON VAN RUYSDAEL (*c.* 1600–70)   Dutch
River Landscape with Boats, c. 1640
Oil on canvas, 41½ × 43⅜ in (105.4 × 110.8 cm)

Under a majestic group of oak trees a boat is moored, bearing a flag and the coat of arms of the city of Amsterdam. Travellers in coaches, on horseback and on foot may be seen next to the boats and sailing ships which have come alongside the bank of the river.

The Dutch landscape painters of the mid-seventeenth century did not see nature as grand and overwhelming; they found their motifs in everyday surroundings. Their paintings do not reflect the mood of the artist; nature is seen objectively and enjoyed for its appearance. Ruysdael has not left us a record of an 'Impression'; the Dutch masters did not paint out of doors but worked in the studio from memory and drawings.

The yellow-brown of the oaks in our picture, contrasting with the delicate modulations of grey in sky and water, or the use of a main motif on one side of the composition balanced by a very small motif on the other: these are devices of picture-making which give forcefulness to Ruysdael's account of everyday life on the river.

Formerly in the collection of Lord Castletown at Upper Ossory, the landscape was acquired in 1933 in London under the terms of the Felton Bequest.

BERNARDO CAVALLINO (1616–1656)   Italian
The Virgin Annunciate, c. 1640
Oil on canvas, 33½ × 17½ in (85.1 × 69.2 cm)

Caravaggio's shadowy, *tenebroso* style, which so obviously informed that of Cavallino, is often thought to be limited to 'commonplace realism'. No one, however, could fail to be moved by the tender ecstasy on Mary's miraculously illuminated features set against the night-dark ground. The Angel of the Annunciation would have formed the companion piece, now lost.

Cavallino's colour harmonies and brush technique are very individual; the brown mantle of the Virgin, overlaid with a fine hatching of thin, light-coloured brushstrokes, takes on an olive tone from contrast with the bluish-

crimson of the dress. The hands, delicately and sensitively modelled, are
held back in tone so that the strongest accent of light lies on the Virgin's
profile, strikingly isolated by the impenetrable shadow on the neck and the
jet-black hair.

Formerly in a private collection in France, the picture was acquired from
London in 1968 under the terms of the Felton Bequest.

ALLAN RAMSAY (1713–1784)   British
Richard Grenville, Second Earl Temple
Oil on canvas, 92 × 59⅝ in (233.6 × 152.1 cm)

Ramsay must have seen Van Dyck's portrait of Charles I, known as *The
King at the Hunt*, since Earl Temple is posed in so noticeably similar a
manner; yet despite this resemblance the two portraits affect us very
differently. While Charles the First, surrounded by animals and servants,

40

picturesquely blends with the play of light on foliage and landscape, Earl Temple, alone, towers against an empty sky, his main support being a giant classical pedestal and column. The majesty sweep of the silver-white lining of his Garter robes, foiled by black cape and hat, superbly fills the picture space. The portrait is one of Ramsay's finest achievements during his term as court painter. Though he was clearly conscious of following in Van Dyck's footsteps, his manner of painting, with its dry impasto and closely detailed illusionism, was formed by his association with Italian contemporaries, among whom Pompeo Batoni cultivated the same cool classicism that characterizes this portrait of Earl Temple.

The picture descended in the family of the sitter to the second Duke of Buckingham and Chandos, and was later in the collection of Mrs Alan Palmer, Farley Hall. It was acquired from London under the terms of the Everard Studley Miller Bequest in 1965.

GIAN BATTISTA TIEPOLO (1696–1770)   Italian
The Banquet of Cleopatra, 1743–44 (see p. 14)
Oil on canvas, 98 × 140¼ in (248.8 × 256.2 cm)

Cleopatra's wager with Mark Antony that she would spend a fortune on a single banquet is a subject rarely treated in painting. Tiepolo found less inspiration in other renderings of the theme than in the festive biblical banquets in sixteenth-century Venetian settings painted by Paolo Veronese. Just as *The Banquet* appears seemingly without precursors, so it had no visible followers: the subject lives in our imagination as Tiepolo created it, just as Don Juan remains forever associated with Mozart's opera.

Tiepolo treated the theme a number of times in the 1740s. The Melbourne *Banquet* was finished for Count Algarotti, who seems to have urged the artist to introduce the sculptures of the sphinx and of Isis and Serapis to lend to the sixteenth-century Venetian setting a touch of historical truth. The picture did not please King Augustus III of Saxony, for whom Algarotti had ordered it, and he banished it to his hunting lodge prior to selling it some twenty years later, when the vogue for Neoclassicism had begun to replace the rococo fantasies of Tiepolo.

The picture was sold at Amsterdam in 1765 and purchased for Catherine II of Russia. Offered on the English art market in 1933, it was acquired under the terms of the Felton Bequest.

JACOPO AMICONI (1675–1752)   Italian
Farinelli and his Friends, c. 1751
Oil on canvas, 68 × 96½ in (172.7 × 245 cm)

A number of people important in the history of music are here assembled in
a 'friendship picture', which Carlo Broschi Farinelli (1705–82), Europe's
most famous castrato singer of the century, commissioned shortly before his
retirement to remind him of his proud days at the Spanish court. Holding a
sheet of music, one of his favourite songs composed by himself, the singer is
accompanied by his dog and his page, whose gaily coloured Hungarian
uniform echoes the rose pink and sky blue in the costumes of Farinelli and of
the soprano Teresa Castellini. On the far left appears Metastasio, the court
poet at Vienna, who wrote many of Farinelli's libretti; his figure has been
copied from another portrait. Farinelli seems also to have invited the painter
to join him; and Amiconi, in his smock, stands with his arm round his
patron's shoulder. Well versed in courtly manners, the protagonists present
themselves with the aplomb of stage performers.

Vernon Lee, Charles Burney and other writers attributed the painting
to Farinelli's Venetian period, but it is clear that it must have been painted in
Spain, since Farinelli wears the order of Calatrava bestowed on him by
Ferdinand VI in 1750.

43

JOSHUA REYNOLDS (1723–1792)   British
Miss Susannah Gale, 1763–64
Oil on canvas, 82 ½ × 46¾ in (209.4 × 118.7 cm)

Both Ramsay's Earl Temple and Reynolds' Miss Gale step out from a
classical portico into the open. Both painters looked to Van Dyck for their
compositions. Yet the different temperaments of the two artists are reflected
in the very conception of their pictures. Earl Temple, in his early forties, is
shown as he was: a mature man in his best years. Susannah Gale, a girl of
fifteen, barely more than a child, has been cast in her adult role as the
daughter and heiress of a wealthy British planter in Jamaica. The shy girl is
posed in the manner of one of the grandest of Van Dyck's portraits of the
Genoese nobility, that of Elena Grimaldi, now in the National Gallery in
Washington. The warm chiaroscuro of the natural setting throws into relief
the tender rose-pink and creamy white of her elegantly ruffled gown. Even
in his seemingly direct portrayals, Reynolds paints a 'conceit', incorporates
an ingenious thought, which deepens our interest in his pictures.

   The portrait remained in the family of the sitter until it was sold in 1872. It
passed into the possession of Bertram Currie, then to Laurence Currie, and
was acquired in London in 1933 under the terms of the Felton Bequest.

THOMAS GAINSBOROUGH (1727–1788)   British
The Rt Hon. Charles Wolfran Cornwall, 1785–86
Oil on canvas, 89 × 58 in (226 × 147.3 cm)

Charles Wolfran Cornwall was Speaker of the House of Commons from
1780 to 1789, and possessed, so a contemporary tells us, 'every physical
quality requisite to ornament the place – a sonorous voice, a manly as well as
imposing figure and a commanding deportment'. An unusual example of
Gainsborough's work, this state portrait invites comparison with Ramsay's
Earl Temple. The standing posture of Earl Temple gives full value to his
elaborate costume; Cornwall's seated pose creates a nonchalant disorder in
his splendidly embroidered robe, and this note of informality has been
retained by the artist: instead of an emblem of his august calling, the Speaker
holds a snuff box in his hand, and in place of the classical column so frequent
in grand-manner portraits, Gainsborough has placed a humble landscape in
a gold frame on the right-hand side. Landscapes did not rank highly in

Reynolds' hierarchy of the categories of painting, but they were Gainsborough's first love. The introduction of such simple and natural tastes into a grand-manner portrait is refreshing.

The portrait remained in the family of the sitter until 1961, when it was acquired under the terms of the Everard Studley Miller Bequest.

JEAN-ANTOINE HOUDON (1741–1828)   French
Jean-Jacques Rousseau, 1778
Plaster bust, h. 15¼ in (38.7 cm)

The combination of truth to nature and rarified form gives to Houdon's heads such singular quality that they outshine all other portrait sculptures of his time. In the Melbourne bust he depicts the famous philosopher *en nudité héroïque*, in Neoclassical simplicity, without the trappings of contemporary wig and jacket. It is a posthumous portrait: on the news of Rousseau's death, Houdon visited his house at Ermenonville to take a death mask, from which he modelled the terracotta of which the plaster is a cast. Nevertheless the head is instinct with the cult of sensibility which Rousseau inspired.

The bust, which was exhibited at the Houdon Centenary at the Galerie Buvelot in Paris in 1928, came from the cabinet of the Marquis de Flamarens; it was subsequently owned by the Marquise de Caussade, and by Madame André Cammoins; it was acquired in London in 1972 under the terms of the Everard Studley Miller Bequest.

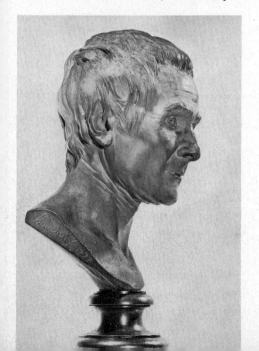

47

John Constable (1776–1837)   British
Study of a Boat Passing a Lock, 1825
Oil on canvas 40$\frac{1}{2}$ × 51$\frac{1}{8}$ in (102.8 × 129.9 cm)

'In some of these subjects of Landscape an attempt has been made to arrest
the more abrupt and transient appearance of the CHIAR'OSCURO IN NATURE;
to shew its effect in the most striking manner, to give "to one brief moment
caught from fleeting time" a lasting and sober existence', wrote John
Constable in the Introduction to *English Landscape* in 1833. The *Study of a
Boat Passing a Lock* is one of a large number of variations on a theme, one of
which was eventually used as the diploma picture for the Royal Academy.
While the foreground, with its moss-covered woodwork, the plants on
which raindrops sparkle, and the boat which is approaching the lock, has the
detailed narrative character of his elaborated paintings, the distance catches
the fleeting effect of sun rays penetrating through clouds; the returning light
brings back pure greens and blue-greens in the distant valley as it stretches
towards Dedham church tower on the horizon. Constable's passionate
interest in the paintings of Claude Lorraine, however, enabled him to give a
lasting and sober existence to narrative and momentary effects; the diagonal
lead-in, the balance held between dark cloud and tree, the off-centre
position of the telling red in the coat of the lock-keeper, are as carefully
calculated as any effect in the work of the classical tradition of landscape.

The picture long remained unknown; it came from a private collection in
Exeter and was acquired on the London art market in 1950 under the terms
of the Felton Bequest.

GUSTAVE COURBET (1819–1877)   French
The Wave, c. 1865–69
Oil on canvas, 20¼ × 28 in (51.4 × 71.1 cm)

In the 1850s Courbet had startled academicians and the public by submitting
to the Salon subjects from the down-to-earth, simple and tough aspects of
life in his own time, instead of the classical, biblical and literary themes
sanctioned by tradition. His realism, however, was different from the
realism of the past. For example, in Holland in the seventeenth century,
Ostade had depicted his peasants carousing; but Courbet's peasants and
workers are involved in dramatic, heroic or pathetic circumstances; his
realism is clearly post-Romantic. His landscapes, many of them inspired by
his passion for deer shooting, are similarly direct and elemental. His *Wave*
series, to which this picture belongs, was anticipated by Whistler in a
painting of breakers. Whistler, however, in the main preferred calm views
with a high horizon, and delicately brushed-in in liquid colours, producing
effects resembling Eastern art; Courbet gave his wave the elemental power
that he admired in peasant life. Though he maintained that 'the beauty
based on nature is superior to all artistic conventions', he employed planes
running parallel with the picture surface, an artful deviation from sym-
metry, and dramatic chiaroscuro effects, all of which are conventions
sanctioned by tradition. With palette knife and brush he worked the paint
into a dense surface of great richness, giving the wave and its foam an
existential presence.

Formerly in the collection of Théodore Duret, this painting was acquired
in London in 1923 under the terms of the Felton Bequest.

CLAUDE OSCAR MONET (1840–1926)   French
Rough Weather at Etretat, c. 1883
Oil on canvas, 25¾ × 31½ in (65.4 × 80 cm)

The brushwork reveals Monet's spontaneous reaction to the visible scene, to
the swirling water, the misty foam, the reddish rock, sparsely dotted with
small plants, and to the marbled effect of light-rimmed clouds. A silvery
grey pervades the sky, water and shore; the pale scene is given scale and
thrown into perspective by the diminutive dark figures in the foreground.
The brushwork varies with the surface of each object; waves, foam, rock
and clouds each have their own texture and subdued mixed tints.

During the 1880s Impressionism passed through a crisis. Renoir and
Pissarro were assailed by doubts about their aims. Pointillism and Post-
Impressionism began to develop. Monet had more and more trouble in
finding methods of working that satisfied him. He gradually systematized
his brushstrokes to the manner which appears in *Vétheuil* (p. 53), and used
colour no longer descriptively but to create an effect of intensity.

The picture was acquired in Paris in 1913 under the terms of the Felton
Bequest.

CAMILLE PISSARRO (1831–1903)   French
Boulevard Montmartre, 1897
Oil on canvas, 28⅞ × 36⅜ in (73.3 × 92.4 cm)

The vision of a world city without motor-cars, traffic-lights and congestion may well appear a lost paradise to the twentieth-century observer. But at least part of the sparkle of the picture is due to the Impressionists' art of presenting subjects as if composed of light.

Pissarro's basic design is classical in its balance, the gaslight in the centre providing the pivot to which attach the two unequal, yet complementary, sides of the composition. Horse-drawn cabs and carts, pedestrians walking amid spindly, wintry trees, kiosks and pillars for posters, are set down in short dabs of broken colours; the high façades with their shopfronts, awnings and balconies lead the eye into the rainy distance. The sparkle and harmony of the whole arises from the way in which colours are worked into a bed of warm grey, providing a continuous web of tone and texture.

Grey was Pissarro's favourite effect; he loved rainy days and overcast skies and once dismissed from his mind a smarting insult with the words: 'Bah, let us work hard and try to make dazzling greys.'

This, the first Impressionist painting to be acquired for Melbourne, was bought, under the terms of the Felton Bequest, from an exhibition held by Durand-Ruel in London in 1905.

EDOUARD MANET (1832–83)   French
House at Rueil, 1882
Oil on canvas, 35¼ × 28¼ in (89.5 × 71.7 cm)

In 1880 Manet contracted an inflammation of the legs which, growing steadily worse, confined him to a wheelchair. In the summer of 1882 he rented the house of Eugène Labiche, the dramatist, at Rueil near Sèvres, and, forced to abandon figure painting, occupied himself with views in the garden and fruits and flowers which his friends sent him.

The square modern building with its grey shutters has been transformed into a luminous backdrop punctuated by the shadowy blue of the window panes. Enhanced by contrast, the greens of the foreground, ranging from dark to the brightest hues, lift the spectator into the light-dappled shadow of a summer garden. Technically this is one of the most Impressionist of all Manet's works. An oblong version, in the Staatliche Museen, Berlin, precedes it.

The picture was previously in the Faure collection, Paris, and the Theodor Behrens collection, Hamburg. It was acquired in London in 1926 under the terms of the Felton Bequest.

CLAUDE OSCAR MONET (1840–1926)   French
Vétheuil, c. 1888
Oil on canvas, 23 × 31 ¼ in (58.4 × 79.4 cm)

'I want to grasp the intangible. It's terrible how the light runs out, taking
colour with it. Colour, any colour, lasts a second, sometimes three or four
minutes at most. What to do, what to paint in three or four minutes?
They're gone, you have to stop. The pain it causes me!' So Monet spoke to
René Gimpel in 1918. The need to capture short moments, in the inexorable
progress of the sun, made him develop a highly disciplined technique which
ensured swiftness. A limited palette of pink, yellow, green and light blue
was used here in dry small brushstrokes placed over a dark-blue ground,
which remains visible between the dabs of paint, and gives resonance to the
light tones. The pink of the sun tinges the clouds, is thrown back from the
roofs and mingles with the reflections of the pale yellow houses and the blue
of the sky in the ripples of the water. The texture of the paint lends a
tapestry-like, decorative quality to the surface, while the brilliance of the
colours symbolizes the dazzle of light.

Another, closely related version, now in Toronto, is dated 1879.

This painting was acquired in 1937 from Durand-Ruel, Paris, under the
terms of the Felton Bequest, and on the advice of Sir Sidney Cockerell.

EDOUARD VUILLARD (1868–1940)   French
Madame Bonnard, 1907
Oil on canvas, 43 × 34 ⅝ in (109.1 × 87.9 cm)

The portrait most delightfully conveys an impression of life being lived, in
the early part of our century, by French people of comfortable middle-class
means. The decorative grid of the canvas has been filled with some sharply
observed reality, such as the absorbed communication between mistress and
dog, which is deftly held in restraint while being offered a titbit. The handling of paint is evocative rather than descriptive, and excels in splendid
colour harmonies, such as the luminous blue and orange of the hat and the
red and green tones of the decoration on the wallpaper and on the armchair.
As Meier-Graefe, the great writer on art of Vuillard's own day, has aptly said
about this artist and other members of his circle, the Nabis: 'We may ask
ourselves which is the greater miracle – the pictures evolved from the
bearish vigour of Courbet, or the harmonies that breathe from the trembling essays of these younger men.'

This portrait was acquired under the terms of the Felton Bequest in
London in 1955.

ROBERT DELAUNAY (1885–1941)   French
Nude Reading, c. 1915
Oil on canvas, 33 $^7/_8$ × 28 $^1/_8$ in (86 × 71.5 cm)

Deeply involved with the problems of Cubism as they appeared in the work
of Picasso and Braque, Delaunay aimed to make of light what the other
artists had made of form: he wanted to make the treatment of light a
creative art form, and to express light through contrasting colours. The
light that falls on the nude here has been organized into oval shapes and
created out of the basic colours of the spectrum. The pearly hues are
contrasted with the stronger colours of the surroundings. Apollinaire gave
this new style the name of Orphic Cubism, thereby reminding us of the
poetic power of colour which transfigures the scene, so that the woman
who reads seems herself changed into poetry.

   Nude Reading was acquired in London under the terms of the Felton
Bequest in 1966.

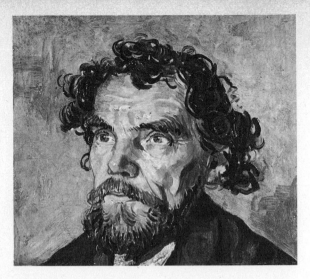

VINCENT VAN GOGH (1853–1890)   Dutch
Head of a Man, c. 1886
Oil on canvas, 12¼ × 15½ in (31.1 × 39.3 cm)

This vivid face was probably painted in Paris, but before Van Gogh had
adopted the brilliant hues of the French Pointillistes. The treatment is almost
monochrome, as in his earlier work. The impetuosity of the brushwork
recalls the manner of Frans Hals. Van Gogh was an incisive draughtsman,
and organized line also dominates his painting; the brushstrokes vividly
model the wings and tip of the nose and weld together forehead and hollow
of the eye by means of the lines of the eyebrows, while strands of hair swirl
like dark flames around the head.

The portrait, formerly in the V. A. Cazalet collection, was purchased in
Melbourne in 1939 from 'The Herald Exhibition of French and British
Contemporary Art'.

ALFRED SISLEY (1840–1899)   French
Straw Ricks, 1891
Oil on canvas, 28 × 35¾ in (71.1 × 90.8 cm)

The reviewer of D. S. McColl's *Nineteenth Century Art* in a Melbourne
journal in 1903 lamented the absence of works by Monet and Manet and
other important nineteenth-century painters from the Melbourne Gallery,
on which by then, so he reminded his readers, the sum of £100,000 had been

spent. Two years later the first work by a French Impressionist went on the walls of the Gallery and by 1913 three such works had been acquired. But it would be hard to point to an immediate impact on local painters. Impressionism of a kind had been the *dernier cri* in Melbourne in the 1880s, when Roberts, Conder and Streeton painted in the open air in their camps around Melbourne. By 1891, when Conder had settled in Paris, he wrote to Tom Roberts in Melbourne: 'I wish you could have seen some of his [Monet's] landscapes: *they lived*, and he does them in the funniest way. He paints a good deal still with pure colour, but you quite lose the paint at three or four yards . . . after all the greatest landscape painter in his way.' Conder did not try to acquire Monet's short stroke technique, but was taken with what was then the newest fashion, Art Nouveau and Symbolism. In Melbourne itself, by 1913, a high-key tonal painting in the open air was opposed by a low-key tonal school, working in the manner of the Barbizon School. Much more noticeable was the interest taken in French Impressionism in the 1960s by the Australian followers of American Abstract Expressionism, who closely scrutinized the handling of paint in the six works by Monet, Sisley and Pissarro in the collection.

This painting was acquired in London in 1913 under the terms of the Felton Bequest.

KAREL APPEL (b. 1921)   Dutch
Moonbird, 1956
Oil on canvas, 38 × 51 ½ in (96.5 × 130.8 cm)

Although made up from the words Copenhagen, Brussels and Amsterdam, COBRA, the name of Appel's early brotherhood of artists, aptly reflects the primitive and savage vehemence which Appel cultivates not only in his technique but in his choice of subjects. We may interpret *Moonbird* as frightening or grotesquely humorous; he may remind us of Sepik River hornbills (see p. 149) or of the ferocity of Kokoschka's *Tiger*; we may compare the technique with the Abstract Expressionism of De Kooning; yet *Moonbird* remains typically Appel's own. The handwriting of the laced brushwork closely resembles the brushwork in his *Tragic Nude* of the same year; the vigorous impasto passages, the close-to-the-surface imagery, the coherence of the composition, which gives the impression of having been carried out at great speed, all are the hallmark of Appel's work of the 1950s.

It was acquired in 1961 in London under the terms of the Felton Bequest.

HELEN FRANKENTHALER (b. 1928)   American
Cape (Provincetown), 1964
Synthetic polymer paint and resin on unprimed canvas, 109⅝ × 93¼ in
(2.78 × 2.37 m)

Abstract Expressionists like Helen Frankenthaler use colour and scale for
impact on the spectator; the large size of *Cape*, together with its cool colour
chords, is like a poem on the vastness of sea and sky. The areas of stained,

unprimed canvas create no third dimension; the eye does not move into the picture space but follows the heavy surface layers which contract into a falling drop; associations of sky, cloud, vegetation and beach form themselves in the mind of the spectator, but the work itself is non-figurative. In marked contrast to the Abstract Expressionists who preceded her, Helen Frankenthaler distinguishes herself by a quiet lyrical mood, which she shares with such contemporaries as Sam Francis.

It was acquired from the exhibition 'Two Decades of American Painting' selected by Waldo Rasmussen of the Museum of Modern Art, New York, and shown in Melbourne in 1967.

AUGUSTE RODIN (1840–1917)   French
Balzac, 1891–98
Bronze, h. 111 in (2.82 m)

When in 1891 Rodin was commissioned by the Société des Gens de Lettres to make a statue in honour of Balzac, the sculptor had never seen his model, since the author had died in 1850. Like a detective, Rodin set about collecting his evidence; but though he studied daguerreotypes, and the native types of Balzac's province (Touraine), though he even had a suit made by Balzac's tailor who still had the writer's measurements, he finally created a symbolic rather than a realistic image. The head has become everything; the great novelist has been represented without any accessories. The amorphous figure only acts as the foil for the imposing head. A decade later, Julius Meier-Graefe, one of the most perceptive writers on art of Rodin's period and a partner in the dealer Bing's Maison de l'Art Nouveau, could claim: 'The *Balzac* belongs to the age as does hardly any other work of art. . . . This distorted face shows the heroism of the conqueror better than could any allegories. It is the only method of representation proper to our age: in those eyes that grow inward, in the shreds and hollows of which this scarcely human face is fashioned, in the grotesque attitude, full of pride and sovereign disdain, the mask of this Caliban, and that which lay behind it, is painted. It is a fabulous symbol; it exaggerates that which should be exaggerated in this case. Ugliness, the proud result of conscious self-destruction, becomes a monument to beauty.'

This cast, one of six made since the death of Rodin, was acquired from the Musée Rodin in Paris in 1968 under the terms of the Felton Bequest.

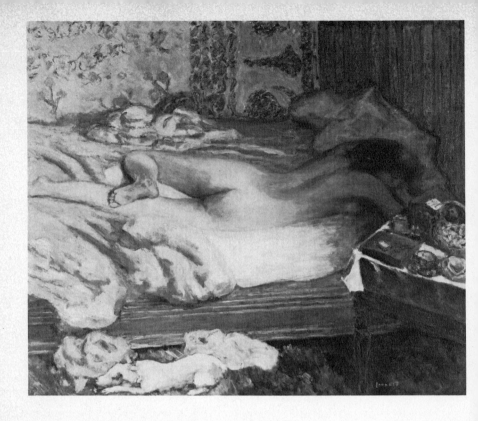

Pierre Bonnard (1867–1947)   French
Siesta – The Artist's Studio, 1907–08
Oil on canvas, 43¹/₈ × 51¹/₄ in (109.5 × 130.1 cm)

In his so-called Nabi period, in the 1890s, Bonnard had made enchantingly
conceived, witty colour lithographs and paintings of aspects of life on the
Parisian boulevards and in its parks, transmuting these mundane scenes into
the simplest shapes, distributed on canvas or paper with all the eccentric
refinement of the *fin de siècle*. About 1900 his work underwent a change; his
colours increased in range, intensity and opaqueness, and he introduced
more observations from reality, surrounding his figures with the setting of
their daily life. He still composed from memory: 'the presence of the object,
the motif', he wrote, 'is very disturbing to the painter at the time he is
painting.' He continued to draw his themes from the casual accidents of life;
the inspiration for this picture is not the model posed for drawing but the
model abandoning herself to relaxation during a hot summer day. The

62

shapes of the bedclothes harmonize with the flowing lines of the body and contrast with the jewel-like colour patterns of wallpaper and studio table. Little touches of humour, such as the miniature poodle having *his* sleep on the rug amid the hastily shed undergarments, contribute to the atmosphere of contented domesticity which suffuses the scene like a perfume.

This work was acquired in London in 1949 under the terms of the Felton Bequest.

AMEDEO MODIGLIANI (1884–1920)   Italian
Portrait of the Painter Manuel Humbert
Oil on canvas, 39$\frac{1}{2}$ × 25$\frac{5}{8}$ in (100.3 × 65 cm)

One of the outstanding characteristics of this Italian painter, who suffered neglect and, ruining his health in dissipation, died an early death, was his unfailing kindness to other artists. Here he portrayed with evident sympathy a young, little-known Spanish painter, who like him had been attracted by the world of Picasso, Brancusi, Lipchitz, Braque and other members of the School of Paris.

With the head close to the upper margin and the hands very low down in the picture space, the picture is a twentieth-century translation of the Mannerist portrait convention of Bronzino, which Modigliani was able to study in his youth in Florence. The articulated narrow space, the solemn frontality of the pose, are handled without surface realism and without modelling except by contour. The outline of the face, the angle of the sharply shaped nose, the lines of the eyebrows, and the rounded contours of the hands, do more to create form than the very slight shading employed around the chin and along the neck. Modigliani was inspired to such formal means by the newly discovered aesthetics of Negro art, and by the work of the Cubist sculptors. He achieves a wistful harmony, reinforced by the sombre beauty of his colours: the glowing orange tones of the face and hands are effectively set off against the warm dark brown of background and figure.

Previously in the collections of L. Zborowski, Paris, and Netter, Paris, the portrait was acquired in London in 1948 under the terms of the Felton Bequest.

GEORGES ROUAULT (1871–1958)   French
Christ on the Veil of St Veronica
Oil on canvas, 28½ × 20¼ in (72.4 × 51.5 cm)

Early medieval religious imagery owed its formalized character to the desire of the craftsman to retain an established tradition and to the limitations created by the nature of the medium he used. Copying directly from nature only made a gradual appearance in later centuries, and fell once more into disfavour after Cubism and Fauvism had brought back conceptual painting. Rouault, concerned with the solemnity and authority of an image sanctioned by a long tradition, creates a face of Christ which has its origin in the stark simplicity of Romanesque carvings and of early Gothic stained glass. The strong black areas framing the face and outlining the features seem inspired by the leading of church windows. The head is shown according to the story of St Veronica, who on the road to Golgotha offered Christ her veil to wipe his brow; the imprint of his face was left on the veil.

The work formerly belonged to Ambroise Vollard, Paris. It was acquired in London in 1951 under the terms of the Felton Bequest.

RENÉ MAGRITTE (1898–1967)   Belgian
In Praise of Dialectics
Oil on canvas, 25 ½ × 21 ¼ in (64.5 × 54 cm)

The movement of Surrealism was one of many attempts of the twentieth
century to free itself from traditional notions of picture making. Magritte
practised a meticulous realism, but the reality he depicts is stood on end. We
approach the window of a house, but we have no ground under our feet.
The window is open and we expect to see a furnished interior. Instead we
are confronted with what we might see if we were inside the room looking
out: a house, as it might stand on the opposite side of the street. Domestic
interiors, their seclusion and the window opening on the infinite world
outside, had been a favourite theme of Romanticism, the nineteenth-
century novement which was one of the targets of attack for the twentieth-
century innovators.

The painting was acquired from London in 1972 under the terms of the
Felton Bequest.

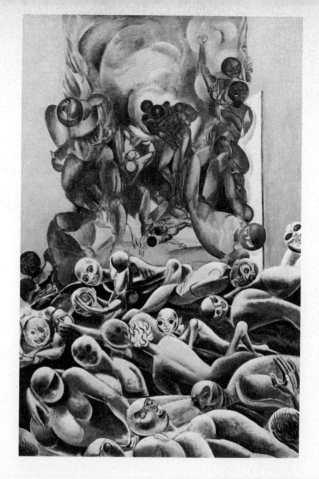

Percy Wyndham Lewis (1884–1957)   British
Inferno, 1937
Oil on canvas, 60 × 40 in (152.4 × 101.6 cm)

An avalanche of damned creatures, red hot from the infernal fires, fall down
to where others, though drained and purged, are nevertheless still haunted
by sensuality. C. Handley Reid has quoted verses from T. S. Eliot's 'Whis-
pers of Immortality' which may well have inspired Lewis:

> Webster was much possessed by death
> And saw the skull beneath the skin;
> And breastless creatures underground
> Leaned backwards with a lipless grin.

Daffodil bulbs instead of balls
Stared from the sockets of the eyes!
He knew that thought clings round dead limbs
Tightening its lusts and luxuries.

Donne, I suppose, was such another
Who found no substitute for sense,
To seize and clutch and penetrate;
Expert beyond experience.

He knew the anguish of the marrow
The ague of the skeleton;
No contact possible to flesh
Allayed the fever of the bone.

This work was acquired under the terms of the Felton Bequest in 1964.

VICTOR VASARELY (b. 1908)   Hungarian-French
Attica
Oil on canvas, 47¼ × 39½ in (120 × 100.3 cm)

As a child Vasarely enjoyed drawing on the steam-clouded double window panes of his home in Hungary and discovered that images superimposed could yield effects of movement. The same effect fascinated him in super-imposed strips of gauze, and such early experiments led him later to develop the optical effects for which he has become famous. In *Attica*, the spectator becomes engrossed in distinguishing between what is in front and what is at the back: does the blue ground come forward or does the black figure stand in front? In fact neither possibility excludes the other, though they may not be experienced simultaneously. Such effects are divorced from will or thought; they appear automatically and give the painter an uncanny power over the viewer. These disquieting events become memorable through taking place within the framework of a beautifully ordered and balanced design and a colour harmony of great refinement.

It was acquired in London under the terms of the Felton Bequest in 1968.

FRANCIS BACON (b. 1910)   British
Study from the Human Body, 1949
Oil on canvas, 58 × 51 ½ in (147.5 × 131 cm)

The monochrome grey, unusual in Bacon's work, is reminiscent of photography, and play with illusion is created by the safety-pin in the curtain
which affects us as the insect, painted by the young Giotto on one of his
master's paintings, affected the latter: we wish to remove it. The illusionist
character of the painting belongs to a time at which Bacon was much
concerned with the work of Velázquez; figure and curtain are interwoven
in a similar way in Bacon's *Study after Velázquez's Pope Innocent X* of 1953.
Bacon has described his manner of painting as 'setting a trap in which one
would be able to catch the fact at its most living point'. The 'fact' is man's
realization 'that he is an accident, that he is a completely futile being'. The
Pope in the *Study after Velázquez* screams. The figure in our painting
appears calm; yet the darkness he steps into, the very fact that it is inexpli-
cable, creates an atmosphere of unease.

    The painting, which was exhibited at the Biennale Internazionale d'Arte,
Venice, in 1954, was acquired in London in 1950.

HENRY MOORE (b. 1898) British
Seated Figure, 1957
Bronze sculpture, h. 73 in (185.4 cm)

To find such monumental seated women in earlier sculpture, one has to go back to classical antiquity, to the Three Fates from the Parthenon, which the artist had studied in the British Museum. Moore achieves a comparable integration of garment and body into a powerful plastic shape. Comparison also makes us aware of the differences: Moore emphasizes the body and reduces the head and limbs in a spirit akin to the creators of archaic Venus figures. The thin arms, the tiny head, the scaly, sheath-like garment, dissociate the figure from the human pathos of the classical tradition which is replaced by an impersonal yet alert energy – a universal life force.

The statue has been cast for use in the open. The folds across the lap are formed like bridges, so that, instead of accumulating, the water can run off underneath them unhindered. The smooth limbs are worked over with freely-drawn lines, providing a durable rather than a highly polished, and hence vulnerable, surface.

This work was acquired from the artist in 1963 under the terms of the Felton Bequest.

DAVID HOCKNEY (b. 1937)   British
Marriage of Styles, 1963
Oil on canvas and collage, 77¾ × 90 in (197.5 × 228.5 cm)

This picture is made in a mixture of painting and assemblage. The format is shaped to suggest a box interior, like a dolls' house. Ready-made wallpaper is brought into effective contrast with the painted scene. The groomed look of the man, with his modish sunglasses, and the lady's sack dress, high heels and long, straight hair, successfully evoke fashions of the 1960s, placed in an up-to-date interior of plate-glass windows, metal frame table with glass top, and cotton-braid mat. Hockney's send-up of Hollywood glamour belongs to the age of the Beatles and of Pop art.

This work was presented by the Contemporary Arts Society, London, in 1965.

PRINTS

ANTONIO POLLAIUOLO (*c.* 1432–1498)   Italian
The Battle of the Nudes, c. 1470
Engraving, $15^{15}/_{16} \times 22^{3}/_{4}$ in (40.4 × 57.8 cm)

In the development of the art of the early Renaissance, sculptors precede
painters in 'the return to the classics and a return to nature'. It is therefore
not surprising that Pollaiuolo, who, as early as 1460–65, had told the story of
Hercules and Antaeus in classical language in his famous bronze figurine
group in the Bargello in Florence, should have been the first to create a
large-scale engraving in which classical form and classical subject-matter are
joined. Since authorities differ in the interpretation of the scene, a variant of
Vasari's title, 'a battle scene', has remained in use. Here we see figures in
stances with which we are acquainted from classical reliefs and vase paintings, but animated beyond classical 'repose' by the muscular detail Pollaiuolo had studied in anatomical dissection. He won Vasari's praise
(apropos of his painting of the *Labours of Hercules*) for 'the venom, the fire,
the fury, all represented with a vigour worthy of admiration and imitation
by all good artists'.

The engraving was previously in the collections of Lord Northwick and
Philip Hofer. It was acquired in London in 1960 under the terms of the
Felton Bequest.

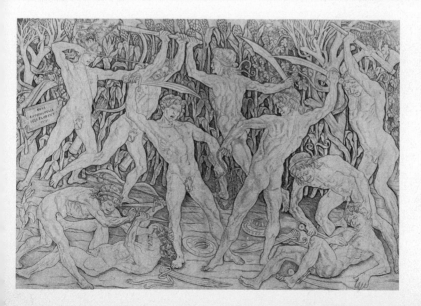

ANDREA MANTEGNA (c. 1431–1506)   Italian
The Battle of the Sea Gods (right half of a frieze)
Engraving, 11 × 15 in (28.9 × 39.6 cm)

In the art of the Middle Ages ancient Greek and Roman gods and demigods
had lost their classical proportions; they had also lost physical presence, since
the medieval artist did not cultivate the ability to depict vigorous action in
an apparently three-dimensional form. In Mantegna's time, the ancient
gods and heroes were restored to the form the artists of classical antiquity
had given them. Mantegna is believed to have illustrated here a legend told
by the historian Diodorus Siculus about a people of fish-eaters (Ichthyo-
phagi); and he has based his figures on Graeco-Roman Nereid sarcophagi
and other antique prototypes, which he imitated with such striking success
that a fifteenth-century terracotta relief (in the Museo Nazionale in Raven-
na), which is based on this engraving, was long regarded as the work from
antiquity which had served as Mantegna's model. The rediscovery of the
pagan past not only supplied early Renaissance artists with models of
perfect, youthful human form, but allowed the vigorous expression of
passions of violence and cruelty without moral censorship.

This engraving was acquired in London in 1965 under the terms of the
Felton Bequest.

74

ALBRECHT DÜRER (1471–1528)   German
The Virgin with the Monkey, 1499
Engraving, 7½ × 4¾ in (19.1 × 12.2 cm)

The Virgin and Child are very similar to those in the popular watercolour
drawing in the Albertina, the *Madonna with the Many Animals*. The clearly
articulated limbs, and particularly the balanced pose of the nude Child,
remind us of figures by the Florentine fifteenth-century painter Lorenzo di
Credi. The paradisaical peace of the scene is conditional on the fettering of
the monkey, the symbol of animal urges. The print shows Dürer's engraving technique at its height: the silvery light and the warm depth of the
shadows are conveyed with the same virtuosity as the surface textures of
wood and fur, the sinuous lines of plants and the evanescence of passing
clouds. This particular impression, one of the earliest of this plate, has the
bull's head watermark of 1499 in the paper. The burr caused by the graver
still carries ink, resulting in the velvety quality of the dark areas. This
impression has frequently been chosen for reproduction, for example by
Campbell Dodgson who chose the best impressions known to him for the
illustrations of his Dürer catalogue.

   From the collections of Dr A. Straeter, Professor Werner Weisbach and
Sir Thomas Barlow, from whom it was acquired under the terms of the
Felton Bequest in 1956.

Rembrandt. f. 1648.

76

REMBRANDT VAN RIJN (1606–1669)   Dutch
Beggars Receiving Alms at the Door of a House, 1648
Etching, $6\frac{1}{2} \times 5\frac{1}{16}$ in (16.5 × 12.9 cm)

Rembrandt rarely used scenes of everyday life in his paintings, and even in
etchings they form only a small part of his *œuvre*, the greater part being
devoted to subjects in which human experience acquires paradigmatic
significance, as in the two Testaments. Even when he deals with a daily
occurrence, the scene conveys a comment on the right life : an old man, well
dressed, receives a group of beggars at his door; he hands them alms. The
old father inclines his head in gratitude while the daughter, burdened with a
baby and another child at her side, eagerly accepts the coin. The view
concentrates on the shadows between the figures; the right-hand side is left
untouched, and calls up the light of the low Dutch sky. The composition is a
simplified version of Rembrandt's *Ratcatcher* of twelve years earlier. The
simplicity of forms and the stillness in which the almsgiving is enacted give a
deep-felt, religious meaning to the episode, with distinguishes Rembrandt's
'genre' from the materially more descriptive and emotionally superficial
genre scenes by the lesser Dutch masters.

A print of exceptional warmth and richness of burr, it was purchased
from the Seymour Haden Collection in 1891.

SAITO SHARAKU (active 1794–after 1825)   Japanese
Matsumoto Yonesaburo, 1794
Colour woodcut, $15\frac{3}{8} \times 10\frac{1}{4}$ in (39 × 26 cm)

Matsumoto Yonesaburo, the No actor, is portrayed here in the role of the
courtesan Kewaizaku no Shosho. Less mask-like than Sharaku's heads of
actors in male roles, this face acquires animation from the exquisite swing of
line of the features and the contour which leads into the calligraphy of the
kimono. The black hair is balanced by the black sash of the dress, above
which emerges the expressive little hand holding a tiny pipe.

The play, performed in 1794, is called *Katakiuchi Noriai Banashi (A Medley
of Tales of Revenge)*. The heroine, preparing to avenge her murdered father,
becomes a courtesan; we have, as it were, a double transformation – the
male actor is disguised as a girl who is disguised as a courtesan.

Little is known about Sharaku, whose actor portraits are among the
rarities of Ukiyo-e prints, an art form which was created for ordinary

people in cities, reflecting the pleasures and amusements of artisans and traders. He was himself a *No* actor, in the troupe of a feudal lord, the Daimyo of Awa: He drew his heads for the printer Tsutaya Jusaburo, who had the blocks cut and the head printed against a shimmering mica ground which strikingly enhances their effect.

This woodcut was acquired in London in 1966 under the terms of the Felton Bequest.

HENRI DE TOULOUSE-LAUTREC (1864–1901)   French
Lender, Half-length, Bowing, 1895
Colour lithograph 12 $^{13}/_{16}$ × 9 $^{3}/_{4}$ in (32.5 × 23.5 cm)

A new chapter in the history of European printmaking begins with the sharp, smart, nervous line, drawn on stone for multiplication, with which Toulouse-Lautrec, adapting hints from Japanese colour prints, immortalized the passing parade of the Parisian 1890s. While other late nineteenth-

78

century artists fled from the urban and industrial scene into the country, to Tahiti, into fantasy, or turned to primitive art, Lautrec betook himself to the popular entertainment places of Paris. The lithograph here was commissioned by the German writer Julius Meier-Graefe for his magazine *Pan*, and depicts the actress in the costume in which she appeared in F. R. Hervé's operetta *Chilpéric*. From a large painting Lautrec made of Mlle Lender dancing the *bolero* in this operetta, one gathers that, while the other participants wore vaguely period (i.e. sixth-century Frankish) costumes, the heroine and her partner were dressed in the Spanish fashion appropriate to their plainly anachronistic performance. Her high-strung, treacherous-looking features, outlined in olive, blue and red and set off by the red hair, the delicate animation of the paper surface by varying patterns of coloured line, the translation of reality into a freely decorative effect, are prophetic of the twentieth century.

This brilliant impression, from the now comparatively rare second state, was purchased in London in 1971. It came from a French private collection.

EDVARD MUNCH (1863–1902)   Norwegian
The Kiss, 1897–1902
Colour woodcut, 18¼ × 18½ in (46.4 × 47 cm)

Munch, who early became a member of the anti-bourgeois naturalist movement, resembles Strindberg in his preoccupation with sex and his distrust of women. During the 1890s women appear in his work as sinister vampire-like creatures, or as unapproachable and dominated by anxieties. His style is Symbolist, and, in woodcut particularly, much inspired by Gauguin. After the obsessive, apprehensive imagery of conflict between the sexes, *The Kiss*, and the variations on this theme, introduce a new note of harmony. In the earliest version, an oil painting of 1897, the face of the woman is hidden by that of the man; in the woodcut, the two faces have melted into one unit; the outline of the group, drawn in a *faux-naïf* manner, has been cut out of its block, and the black print from it has been overprinted with another block, the marked grain of which gives the work a twentieth-century look. The mixture of simplified drawing and pre-existing *objet trouvé* effect has retained its appeal from German Expressionism to westernized Japanese printmaking and to the late Abstract Expressionism of the 1960s.

This woodcut was acquired in 1948 under the terms of the Felton Bequest.

PIERRE BONNARD (1867–1947)   French
Four-panel Screen, 1899
Four five-colour lithographs, each 57½ × 17½ in (146 × 44.5 cm); total
size 57⅞ × 73¼ in (147 × 186 cm)

Bonnard's chosen nickname, as a member of the Nabi group in the 1890s,
was *Nabi Japonard*; and he was clearly inspired to the use of the screen form
by the Japanese sexpartite screens which could be seen in Paris in private
collections, as well as at Samuel Bing's shop L'Art Nouveau. The composition, which places the main shapes outside the centre and balances them by
empty areas, shows, as Heinz Spielmann suggests, that Bonnard must have
known paintings by Ogata Korin (1658–1716) or his school. The subjects
depicted, however, are purely Parisian, as they could have been observed in
any park or on the boulevards. The ornamental row of horses and coaches at
the top is conceived in the style of Art Nouveau. The costume of the maid is
very similar to that in the poster for the *Revue Blanche*. Displaying a close
observation of life, the figures are not only superbly placed but most
economically and decoratively formalized.

The work was published by Malines, Paris, in an edition of 110. This
impression was acquired in London in 1946 under the terms of the Felton
Bequest.

DRAWINGS

FLORENTINE SCHOOL   Italian
Eight Famous Men, c. 1450
Pen, ink and coloured washes on vellum, 12 $^3/_8$ × 7 $^7/_8$ in (31.4 × 20 cm)

The page comes from a picture chronicle with illustrations of famous men from the Six Ages of the World, of which, according to medieval historians, history was composed. From left to right, they are: Pyrrhus son of Achilles, Ascanius son of Aeneas, the Prophet Samuel, King Eurythames of Sparta, King Codrus of Athens, King Aletes of Corinth, David, and Absalom. Figures taken from the 'Fourth Age' of classical and biblical antiquity, they are, in the customary medieval manner, garbed in the dress of the painter's own time, yet they have a bodily presence and firmness of stance that distinguishes them from Gothicism. The simple outlines, the shading and colouring, bear a marked resemblance to the work of Piero della Francesca, but it is not known who the artist was. Series of famous men continued to be painted, sculpted and engraved until recent times, but the fantasy element of the sequence here was soon abandoned for greater historical accuracy. Renaissance artists began to rely on actual portrait likenesses for such sequences. The most celebrated portraits of famous men occur in Van Dyck's *Iconography*, mainly dating from 1634–35, the 'Landau-Finaly' set of which is in the Print Room Collection.

The chronicle came from a French collection and was successively owned by William Morris, Charles Fairfax Murray and Sir Sydney Cockerell. It was broken up and dispersed at the Sotheby sale of 2 July 1958. The page here was acquired in London in 1966 under the terms of the Felton Bequest.

ANDREA DEL SARTO (1486–1531)   Italian
Study of St John the Baptist
Drawing, sanguine, 12 $^3/_8$ × 7 $^5/_{16}$ in (31.4 × 18.6 cm)

Andrea del Sarto worked in Florence at the time when Raphael and Michelangelo were active in Rome. He was to a great extent a follower of Raphael, but in 1516 Michelangelo returned to Florence, and in the frescoes in the Chiostro dello Scalso, for one of which the *St John* is a study, Andrea shows a sudden preoccupation with Michelangelo's figure motifs.

The stance of St John is derived from Michelangelo's *St Matthew*, and the lean muscular limbs, the energetic turning of forms, the swelling contours, are in the great master's spirit. True to the practice introduced by the Renaissance, the figure is studied from the nude model, the fall of the mantle being indicated briefly by a few sweeping lines.

The drawing has been frequently reproduced, among other places in the Vasari Society folios, and was exhibited in 1930 at the Italian exhibition at Burlington House in London. It belonged successively to the collectors Lechevallier-Chevignard, J. P. Heseltine and Henry Oppenheimer, and was acquired in 1936 under the terms of the Felton Bequest.

ANNIBALE CARRACCI (1560–1609)   Italian
Nude Male Figure
Black chalk on grey paper, $14^7/_8 \times 17^7/_8$ in (37.7 × 32.8 cm)

This study for one of the supporting figures on the ceiling of the gallery at the Palazzo Farnese in Rome is a masterpiece of draughtsmanship. Based on the garland-bearing youths of the Sistine Chapel ceiling, and standing in an attitude resembling Michelangelo's Jonah, the figure reminds the spectator that Annibale aimed to revive the artistic principles of his great predecessor.

With typically Baroque irony, the artist expects us to relish the contrast between the Sistine ceiling decorations, in a Vatican chapel, and his own in a secular interior. Michelangelo's subject had been the Creation of the World and Man's Fall from Grace. Annibale's ceiling celebrates the power of earthly love. In the finished work this majestic youth turns his glance towards a depiction of the loves of Venus and Anchises. The splendid drawing is closely studied from the model, but the resulting figure has been magnified and purified in the spirit of the great art of the past.

Once in the collection of Sir Thomas Lawrence, this drawing formed part of the Earl of Ellesmere's group of Carracci drawings which were sold at Sotheby's in 1972.

BYZANTINE SCHOOL   Greek
Theophanes Offering his Work to the Virgin, c. 1100
Illumination on vellum, page size 9½ × 6¾ in (24.2 × 16.5 cm)

At first glance this frontispiece to the Gospels, depicting the scribe and illuminator before the Virgin, bears a marked resemblance to the enamels of the Limoges casket. The blue, green, red, gold splendour of the colour scheme, the flattened figures and ornaments, have a distinct family likeness.

85

Yet the two works are examples of two quite distinct phases in the development of Western art. (See p. 142.)

In the illumination, the art inherited by the Byzantine masters from their Graeco-Roman forerunners has been attenuated and etherealized; the shimmering gold ground replaces tangible space; the architecture has been reduced to a flat decoration, and on the almost bodiless, elongated figures areas of light and grooves of shade suggest folds. Though the background space is flat, the Virgin occupies a platform diagonally receding into a space which is not there. The Limoges enamel contains no such ambiguities. The graphic incisions on the garments convey the idea, but not the illusion, of folds. The flat, blue ground is solid surface, which holds no suggestion of depth. The figures are part of the surface, starkly defined by their outline, and stand or sit before, rather than within, the ground. Not surprisingly, perhaps, the art of Byzantium retained many more of the basic illusionist features of the Ancient Greek tradition than did the art of the French Romanesque at Limoges.

The Gospel Book had been in the collections of the Duke of Hamilton, the Prussian State Library, Charles Fairfax Murray and C. W. Dyson Perrison before it was acquired under the terms of the Felton Bequest in 1959.

SAFAVID DYNASTY (16th century)   Persian
Siyavosh Undergoes the Ordeal of Fire
Book illumination on paper, $8^{1}/_{8} \times 7^{5}/_{16}$ in (20.6 × 18.5 cm)

The heroic age of Persian culture was the Sassanian period; later generations constantly looked back to it. The *Shah Namah*, or Book of Kings, relates the deeds of the early rulers; poets and painters constantly repeated the picturesque legends in this and similar collections. The illumination of Siyavosh,

made after Persian art had reached its maturity, illustrates an episode from the *Shah Namah*. Having failed to seduce him, Siyavosh's stepmother maliciously accused him of attempted rape. He proved his innocence by riding unharmed between two burning piles of wood. In the characteristic Persian tradition, the scene takes place on a rising hillside, which is silhouetted against a gold ground. The Persian artist does not represent space or shadow; the exquisitely delineated detail is flat and combines into a balanced pattern of shapes and colours. The polished surface of the paper and the exquisitely enamelled colours give a preciousness and luxuriance to the page, which speaks of its aristocratic patrons.

The page was acquired from Monif in New York in 1947 under the terms of the Felton Bequest.

JACQUES DE GHEIJN II (1565–1627)   Dutch
Head of a Youth
Pen and sepia ink, $4\,^7/_8 \times 4\,^5/_{16}$ in (12.4 × 11 cm)

Next to the nude, the study of the head was the most important task of the Renaissance draughtsman, since, according to Leonardo, the good artist had to represent 'man and his soul'. Contrasting with the timid, static head drawings made by the medieval Flemish painters, De Gheijn's head is informed by the ideals of the southern Renaissance. The small scale, however, and the precision of the line work, reveal that he was trained as an engraver. The lively duet of the pen, the contrast created by the close detail of the head, the open, free-flowing indication of collar and shoulder, and the freshness of expression, are prophetic of Rembrandt. De Gheijn studied this

attractive head from a living model who sat for quite a number of his drawings.

The drawing was in the collection of C. van der Voordt Pieck (1837), Schretlen and Dr H.C. Valkema Blouw (1945), and was acquired from London under the terms of the Felton Bequest 1958.

REMBRANDT VAN RIJN (1606–1669)   Dutch
Study of an Old Man with Turban
Reed pen and bistre, 6¾ × 5¼ in (17.1 × 13.3 cm)

Religious subjects had little place among the paintings fashionable in seventeenth-century Holland. Protestant churches did not commission altarpieces, and Protestant burghers did not order devotional pictures for their houses. It was largely due to Rembrandt that biblical subjects came to be thought of, as they often were in southern countries, as 'history subjects', pictures intended to 'teach, delight and move'. The effect of Rembrandt's paintings of Susannah and the Elders (now at The Hague and in Berlin), to which our drawing is related, depends on the ability of these works to move our sympathy with the defenceless young girl exposed to two threatening elderly males. The Elder in the drawing here, with his curious hand gesture and pitiless face, his expression of stealth and withheld excitement, is brilliantly lifted from dark shadow created by the broad strokes of the pen.

The drawing was exhibited in the 'Dutch Art' exhibition at Burlington House in 1929 and came successively from the collections of Benjamin West, Sir Thomas Lawrence, W. Esdaile, C.S. Bale, and J.P. Heseltine to Henry Oppenheimer, from whom it was acquired in 1936 under the terms of the Felton Bequest.

J. M. W. TURNER (1775–1851)   British
Red Rigi (Rigi at Sunset), 1842
Watercolour, 18 × 11¾ in (45.7 × 29.9 cm)

This drawing once belonged to John Ruskin, who saw 'in the Red Rigi such a piece of colour as had never come my way before'. It belongs indeed to Turner's latest and finest phase. This *Rigi at Sunset* had as its counterpart *Rigi at Sunrise* (known as the *Blue Rigi*). It was painted in London from drawings and notes made on the spot during Turner's visit to Switzerland in the previous year. With the finest stippling, rubbing, washing and re-touching, Turner achieved an incomparable effect of the immensity of nature and of the interweaving of swirling mists and light. As in Chinese landscape paintings, human beings are dwarfed by the grandeur of the spectacle of nature.

Bought from Turner by H. A. J. Munro, the drawing passed to Ruskin, and to several private collections thereafter. It was acquired in London in 1947 under the terms of the Felton Bequest.

WILLIAM BLAKE (1757–1827)   British
Antaeus, 1824–27
Watercolour, 20 × 14 in (50.8 × 35.5 cm)

Towards the end of their journey through the Inferno, Dante and Virgil are assisted by the giant Antaeus, who sets them down on the ninth and lowest rung of Hell. Some English eighteenth-century writers, such as Thomas Wharton, had taken exception to such unreal scenes as being improper and absurd. Thomas Gray, however, thought it an advantage to Dante's genius 'to have been produced in a rude age of strong and uncontrolled passions when the muse was not checked by refinement'. Blake, in his figure of the giant, has created an image which wonderfully combines a certain primitivism with a sophisticated pose, derived from Tibaldi's Mannerist image of God the Father; by flattening the figure, and by emphasizing its larger-than-life quality, he gives it a barbaric grandeur. Albert S. Roe (author of *Blake's Illustrations to the Divine Comedy*, Princeton 1953) believes that Blake regarded Antaeus as the embodiment of man's physical nature, and that he is therefore divided by a roll of cloud from the eternal world of the imagination, here personified by the two poets. Blake, who despised oil paint and the illusionism to which it lends itself, used watercolour with a fullness and purity of tone not seen again until Turner's work of the 1840s. The strong blue, which surrounds Antaeus, is enhanced by contrast with the reddish-grey note of his body and touches of pink, grey, yellow and green in the surrounding cloud. Like many of these series, this watercolour remained unfinished; Blake died before he could complete this task.

Part of the same series as *Dante Fleeing from the Three Beasts*.

WILLIAM BLAKE (1757–1827)   British
Dante Fleeing from the Three Beasts, 1824–27
Watercolour, 14 × 20 in (35.5 × 50.8 cm)

In a highly rational age Blake believed that art addresses itself to the imagination; his last great undertaking was a series of one hundred plates illustrating that supreme imaginative poem, Dante's *Divine Comedy*. Like Coleridge and Shelley, Blake understood the Divine Comedy as a spiritual journey of the soul through various 'States'. As is usual in Blake, his imagery arises out of his memory of other works of art. A fifteenth-century Venetian woodcut and a number of classical and Gothic sculptures have inspired this illustration to the first canto of the *Divine Comedy*; but these sources have been transformed into a uniquely Blakian image. The absence of realistic details in the highly formalized animals, the dance-like stances of

the fleeing Dante and the rescuer Virgil, impress on the spectator that he is looking at an allegory: Dante flees from the symbols of lust (leopard), ambition (lion) and greed (wolf), and is rescued by Virgil, a Christ-like figure, whose mission it is to lead him on his journey through Inferno, Purgatory and Paradise, towards the recognition of his true self.

Blake's illustrations to the *Divine Comedy*, which had been commissioned by his friend John Linnell, remained in the Linnell family until 1918 when the set was dispersed in London and thirty-six of the watercolours were acquired by the Gallery under the terms of the Felton Bequest.

GIAN BATTISTA TIEPOLO (1696–1770)   Italian
A Scene of Baptism, c. 1742
Pen and bistre wash, 12¾ × 10½ in (32.4 × 26.7 cm)

A patriarch baptizes a kneeling woman and holds his ring for her to kiss; bystanders crowd around; and some metal dishes lie on the ground. The subject has remained unidentified but is probably an Early Christian baptism. Tiepolo, the greatest Italian draughtsman of the Rococo period, worked with a fastidiously restricted range of means, in such a way that a blaze of light seems to emanate from his page. The volume of the figures is indicated by one thin, transparent layer of wash, reinforced by sparsely used

93

deep shadows, the calligraphy of which has the rhythm of rocaille ornament. Very light penstrokes add to the definition of form and detail.

The page was formerly in the collection of Sir Lionel Lindsay
(1874–1962) in Sydney and was acquired in 1962 under the terms of the
Felton Bequest. Its previous history is unknown.

FRANÇOIS BOUCHER (1703–1770)   French
Madame de Pompadour, 1754
Pastel on buff paper, 14½ × 10½ in (36.8 × 26.7 cm)

A decorative *aperçu*, this portrait of Madame de Pompadour superbly
illustrates the taste of the Rococo, both by the pretty, gay and playful

subject and by the serpentine curves and asymmetry of the design. Precariously balancing the weight of their chubby bodies on a frail support, three *putti* cling to a medallion bust portrait of the sitter, which they have decorated with flowers. The emblems of Madame de Pompadour's interest in the arts lie below. A consummate draughtsman, Boucher has used the pastel as a drawing technique. Only the likeness of the Marquise has the high finish that suggests a painting. The remainder of the design is carried out in open line work with a minimum of wiping; the buff ground provides the middle tones, white being used for the highlights. Touches of delicate pink, light blue and emerald green add enchantment to the graceful design, which reveals Boucher's admiration for the work of Rubens.

The pastel was made for the brother of the sitter, the Marquis de Ménars et Marigny; it later went through the collections of Edouard Kahn, Paris, and H. E. ten Cate, Netherlands, and was acquired in 1965 under the terms of the Everard Studley Miller Bequest from Messrs Boerner in Düsseldorf.

THOMAS GAINSBOROUGH (1727–1788)   British
Upland Landscape with Market Cart, Cottage and Figures, 1778
Pen in grey wash and white heightening, 10 $^9/_{16}$ × 13 $^5/_8$ in (26.8 × 33.8 cm)

Gainsborough in his mature years insisted that landscape subjects as well as figures 'must be of his own brain'. 'With regard to real views from Nature in this country', he wrote, 'he has never seen any place that affords a subject equal to the poorest imitations of Gasper [Gaspard Dughet] or Claude'. In the drawing here he is taking up a subject he admired in the painting of Rubens, namely a cart going through a landscape. A Rousseauesque love of the 'simple life' animates the scene, in which, under alternating light and shade amid feathery trees, some cottagers receive their daily supplies from the market woman in her cart. The style connects this drawing with the *Landscape with Horse and Cart* at Althorp.

The drawing was formerly in the collections of W. Esdaile (1840), Dr Th. Monro (1833), Th. Thane (1846), and Sir Thomas Barlow, who presented it in 1950.

HOKUSAI (1760–1849)   Japanese
Old Man Singing to the Accompaniment of a Samisen played by a Girl, 1840–49
Wash drawing, black ink, 9 × 11 ⁵/₈ in (22.8 × 29.5 cm)

The simple theme is presented with a virtuoso variety of expressive
brushstrokes: the broad washes and the lost profile of the old man set off the
varied strokes which portray the girl, who looks at the spectator out of
pinpoint eyes with raised eyebrows, and whose flat Asian nose is succinctly
suggested by a pair of small triangles. No artist before Hokusai had taken
such notice of the small incidents of everyday life. With his tremendous
wealth of observation and his powers of imparting life and movement to his
figures, he introduced a new phase of Ukiyo-e art. His rapid and evocative
brushstrokes remind the western observer of Rembrandt and Goya, with
whom he surely must rank as one of the greatest draughtsmen of all time.
The drawing is one page of seven from a sketchbook, all of which contain
figures which recur on a sheet of studies in the Freer Gallery, Washington.

The sheet here was in an Italian private collection and was acquired in
London in 1966 under the terms of the Felton Bequest.

PAUL KLEE (1879–1940)   Swiss–German
Thistle Picture, 1924
Gouache on linen, 25 × 31 in (63.5 × 78.7 cm)

Paul Klee once compared the artist to the trunk of a tree: 'through the root
the sap flows through the artist, flows through him, flows to his eye'. Instead
of 'the artist as genius', we have the artist as a humble transmitter of powers
inherent in nature. He wanted his pictures to consist of 'the pure structure of
good elements'. His free association, leading from a plant to a bell, to a
ladder and platform, while a bellows shape with the face of a sprite hovers
above, has the logic of dreams and of childhood fantasies. The delicate grey
tones reinforce the shapes against the ground and create a kind of shallow
space, similar to that in Chinese paintings.

The picture was acquired in London in 1952 under the terms of the Felton
Bequest.

MARC CHAGALL (b. 1887)   Russian
Lion and Rat, 1926
Gouache on paper, 25 × 31 in (63.5 × 78.7 cm)

In contrast to most of the masters of the school of Paris, Chagall, who settled
there in 1923, remained attached to storytelling, and to themes from
literature. Retaining an imaginative, Romantic, figurative repertoire of

forms, he absorbed from Cubism its narrow space and tilted planes, but used brilliant colour expressionistically. He is not a literal illustrator; his hundred gouaches to La Fontaine's poems are free variations on the themes of the fables. The rat which gnawed through the net to free the lion is barely visible. Our attention is riveted on the tail-lashing vitality of the lion and the fairy-tale richness of hues; the net, which glows red to emphasize the lion's anguish, is set off by the bordering violet and black areas. Ambroise Vollard, the publisher and dealer, had commissioned the series so that it should be turned into colour lithographs, but the scheme was abandoned and Chagall, some years later, created a series of etchings on the same themes.

It was acquired from the Leicester Galleries, London, in 1952 under the terms of the Felton Bequest.

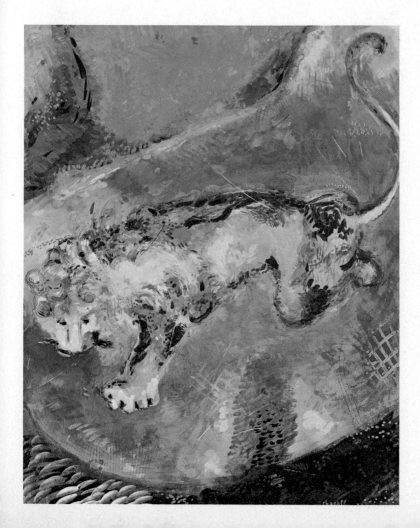

HONORÉ DAUMIER (1808–1879)   French
Two Advocates
Crayon, pen and wash, watercolour and gouache, $11\,^5/_{16} \times 8\,^7/_8$ in
(28 × 21 cm)

Daumier, for the greater part of his life, did cartoon work for journals in
order to stave off want. He was one of the great painters of his day, but
poverty left him little time for it. He was both a realist and a Romantic. In
Don Quixote Reading (also in the Gallery) he depicted the embodiment of the
Romantic artist who rejects ordinary life. The watercolour here deals with
the theme of lawyers – *Gens de Justice* – who formed the subject for many of
his bitterly satirical cartoons, but of whom he also painted scenes such as this,
which were sold independently. The two advocates, passing in the grey
corridors of the law courts, greet each other with exaggerated politeness,
which is made ridiculous by the knowledge that they have perhaps torn a
mutual client to pieces just minutes before. Daumier had been in court
himself, for caricaturing King Louis-Philippe as a pear (*poire* meaning also
'fathead'), and knew from bitter experience the feelings of the victim of a
justice without mercy.

The drawing was in the Cyrus L. Lawrence collection and was acquired
in London under the terms of the Felton Bequest in 1922.

EDGAR DEGAS (1834–1917)   French
Dancer, c. 1880
Brown pastel with touches of colour, 19 × 24¼ in (48.2 × 61.6 cm)

Degas abandoned the classical conventions of figure representation, which
demanded a view from eye-level and a near complete rendering of the
figure. The dancer here is seen from above, bent over so as to be folded in
half, in a pose obscuring the juncture of body and legs. Yet nothing could
convey more forcefully the litheness and strength of the muscular little
figure. Degas had been encouraged by Japanese prints to adopt a form of
composition which balances on a diagonal, and in which figuration and
empty space are given equal weight. The dancer, bent over to tie the ribbon
of her shoe, appears in a number of other works. A charming *Frieze of
Dancers* in Cleveland consists of four variations on the theme, arranged in
the narrow oblong format of Oriental scrolls. *The Rehearsal Room* in the
Metropolitan Museum, New York, equally eccentric in arrangement, has
the Melbourne *Dancer* as its main figure. The aesthetic effect of these
exquisitely composed works is pointed up by the startling unconventional-
ity of the pose.

The drawing was previously in the collections of Sir Robert Abdy and
Captain Victor Cazalet, London, and was acquired in 1938 under the terms
of the Felton Bequest.

PABLO PICASSO (b. 1881)   Spanish
Woman with Fan, 1904
Pen and brown ink, 12¾ × 9¾ in (32 × 24.8 cm)

One of the great masters of drawing, Picasso showed his remarkable
sureness already in his formative period. The study here was made at a time
when, returning to Paris from Spain, he gradually abandoned the melan-
choly poetry of the Blue Period and searched for new motifs among the
habitués of the cafés of Montmartre. Here he records the plumes adorning
the hat of a fashionable lady, her modish air, as well as the graceful gestures
of her hands. A painting of the following year, of a now hatless and timeless
girl, holding the fan and raising the other hand in a dance-like gesture, drew
its inspiration from this study. These drawings are contemporary with *Les
Saltimbanques* and the series devoted to acrobats. The delicate women recall
the Tanagra figures, and the drawings on white-ground Greek vases, which
Picasso admired in the collections of the Louvre. Though the modishness of
Woman with Fan reveals the influence of Toulouse-Lautrec, Picasso retained
a taste for classical restraint and regularity of form which fills this design
with reposeful beauty.

This work was acquired in London in 1968 under the terms of the Felton Bequest.

Sam Francis (b. 1923)   American
Blue, Red and Yellow, 1964
Gouache, 22½ × 30 in (57.2 × 76.2 cm)

The large, bright-blue stains, connected by a filigree of supporting colours, form a pattern of which the white paper remains an active component. The free harmony of the bright, pure hues transmits a sense of joy to the spectator.

A Californian, the artist moved to Paris in 1950 where he became interested in the work of Riopelle, the late Monet, Bonnard and Matisse. His art developed from the particular properties of his medium. Strong colour, the ability to drip and superimpose, the stain quality of the water medium, are exploited for free colour arrangements which suggest nothing but themselves.

This work was acquired in 1966 under the terms of the Felton Bequest.

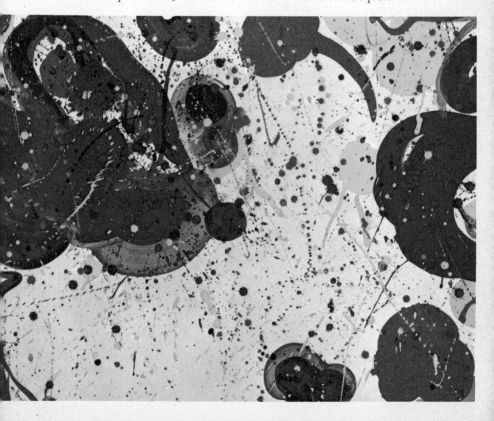

ASIAN ART

NEOLITHIC PERIOD (3500–2000 B C)   Chinese
Pan Shan Mortuary Urn
Pottery, decorated in dark and light brown on buff ground, h. 14¼ in
(36.2 cm)

This urn, which bears a close resemblance to vessels found on grave sites in
Pan Shan in the Province of Kansu, was destined to be filled with bones and
ashes for insertion in a grave; it is left undecorated on the lower half, where
it would have sat in earth or sand. The upper half carries an abstract pattern
consisting of large joined spirals in broad bands of black, lined with dark red
or purple surrounding gourd-shaped figures hatched in black. Similar
painted ware appears in other centres of Neolithic culture, a period in which
people made pottery, used stone tools, domesticated animals and cultivated
cereals. The dynamic rhythm of the pattern, enhancing the form on which
it is painted, and conveying the natural movement of the brush, makes a
powerful impact, but the meaning it may have had is no longer known.

The urn was acquired in 1947 under the terms of the Felton Bequest.

Late Shang or Early Western Chou Dynasty (late 11th century B C)
Chinese

Ting (food vessel)
Bronze with patination, h. 7¾ in (19.5 cm)

The square *ting* is one of the many shapes of ritual vessels in use in the early period for the heating of food over a fire during sacrificial rites. The four legs of the *ting* can straddle the fire and the strong handles allow the hot vessel to be lifted off by means of an instrument. This very fine piece is decorated with *k'uei* dragons above an open panel which is surrounded by rows of nipples.

Acquired in London under the terms of the Felton Bequest, 1964.

HAN DYNASTY (206 BC–AD 221)   Chinese
Horse
Earthenware, h. 12¼ in (31 cm)

The primitive Chinese practice of immolating relatives, servants and animals at the death of heads of households gave way to the use of wooden
substitutes, and during the Han period these wooden grave figures were
replaced by terracotta ones. Part of the attempt to pacify the dead and
prevent them from returning was to give them everything they enjoyed or
would have enjoyed during their lifetime. One of the favoured possessions
of Han dynasty people was the short, deep-chested horse of central Asian
stock, which the Chinese had taken from the Nomad tribes and effectively
used against them. Such a horse is portrayed here with humour and affec-
tion, and with the Chinese craftsman's wonderful ability to convey animal
prowess by the swelling curves of chest and neck, hindquarters and tail.

Part of the collection of Chinese art made by W. H. Kent, it was presented
in 1938.

T'ang Dynasty (AD 618–906)   Chinese
Tomb Figure of a Horse
Glazed pottery, h. 19 in (48.3 cm)

The horse continued to hold a high place in the estimation of the emperors and nobles of the splendid T'ang dynasty. Painters often recorded the favourites of the emperor's stables. Their high standard of observation transmitted itself to the craftsmen who made the grave sculptures; the muscles and bone structure of this horse are as remarkable as the vivacity of its stance. The glazed colours consist of the typical T'ang range of brown, green and yellow. The dull pink of the saddle, which has been left unglazed, throws into relief the brown gloss of the horse's coat.

It was acquired in London under the terms of the Felton Bequest in 1926.

NORTHERN CH'I DYNASTY (AD 550–577)   Chinese
Bodhisattva Mahasthamaprapta
Stone, h. 61 in (155 cm)

This Bodhisattva and its companion, Avalokitesvara, would originally have
stood on either side of a Buddha. Buddhist sculpture was first created in
Gandhara in India, in the second and third centuries AD, where Indian and
Graeco-Roman styles mixed. Large-scale figure sculpture was brought to
China from India in Buddhist examples. In the figure here the human body
has been simplified to a near cylindrical form; following Indian practice, the
Bodhisattva is neither male nor female. Its body, massive without being
sensuous, is hung with heavy chains of jewellery. The features are relaxed, as
in a trance, and the forward-leaning pose suggests powers of levitation.
Holding the vase of the elixir of eternal life and the lotus bud of purity, the
Bodhisattva conveys an impression both majestic and austere. This statue
and its companion are believed to have come from the cave temples of Nan
Hsiang-t'ang in Northern Honan and from the same workshop as the
Bodhisattva in the University Museum, Philadelphia.

    From the collection of Charles Vignier in Paris, it was acquired for the
Felton Bequest in 1956.

T'ANG DYNASTY (AD 618–906)   Chinese
Dancing Girls and Musicians
Terracotta, painted, h. (l. to r.) 7½ in (19.6 cm), 9¾ in (24.8 cm), 10⅞ in
(27.6 cm), 10½ in (26.7 cm)

The grave wares of the T'ang dynasty candidly reflect the varied enjoy-
ments of life, represented with a sure instinct for simplification. Much of the
soft delicacy of the figures here is due to their being unglazed, the hand
colouring added after firing having largely disappeared, but the telling
effect of the sinuous contours is an essential element in the Chinese feeling
for form. The group recalls some lines from a poem by Chang Hêng (AD
78–139), in a translation by Arthur Waley:

                     Up rose the fair ones to the dance
                     Well painted and appareled,
                     in veils of soft gossamer . . .

They have raised their long sleeves, they have covered their eyes;
Slowly their shrill voices
Swell the steady song . . .

Now flutter their cuffs like a great bird in flight,
Now toss their white sleeves like whirling snow.

Part of the W.H. Kent collection, presented in 1938.

SUNG DYNASTY (AD 960–1279)   Chinese
Seated Kuan-yin
Plastered and polychromed wood, h. 43½ in (110.5 cm)

In one of the many forms assumed by this deity, the Bodhisattva Kuan-yin
dispenses mercy; she was thought to live in a weathered grotto on an island
in the Indian Ocean. Our statue may originally have been supported by a
rock-like throne, set in a niche formed by an intricate rockery. Such a
setting, together with the figure's customary adornments of crown and
earrings, now lost, and the richness of colour, now largely rubbed off,
would have resulted in an effect of majestic splendour.

Large-scale figure sculpture was brought to China by Buddhism, as was
the religious emphasis on meditation. The Kuan-yin's right arm is stretched

out towards those who need help and consolation. The face expresses a withdrawal into contemplation. She sits in the pose, developed from one known as 'Royal Ease', traditional for this Bodhisattva. With its smoothly rounded face and arms, and the soft fall of the attire, enlivened by scarves and jewelled chains, the statue, instinct with feminine dignity, has that exquisiteness of line and form characteristic of the art of the Sung and very early Ming Dynasties.

It was acquired in London in 1939 under the terms of the Felton Bequest.

SOUTHERN SUNG DYNASTY (AD 1128–1279)   Chinese
Kinuta Vase
Lung ch'üan celadon, h. 10½ in (26.5 cm)

This felspatic stoneware had its origin in a whole group of pre-Sung celadons made in the province of Chekiang. Its glaze may range in colour from grey through olive-green to brown. The name was coined in Europe and is believed to be taken from Céladon, a shepherd dressed in green who appeared in a play called *L'Astrée*, first produced in Paris in 1610. Chinese collectors refer to it as *ch'ing tz'u* (blue-green porcelain). The finest celadons of the Sung period were made at the kilns of Lung-ch'üan. *Kinuta* is Japanese and means 'mallet'; the term derives from a famous vase of this shape in Japan and is intended to cover all the small class of pieces of outstanding quality with a strongly bluish tint in the glaze, which is dense and close fitting, unctuous and smooth. Adorned with fish-shaped handles, the vase illustrated here is a particularly fine example of this kind of ware.

Part of the W. H. Kent Gift of Chinese Art presented in 1938.

MING DYNASTY (AD 1368–1644)   Chinese
Vase, 15th century
T'zu Chou ware, with dark-brown drawing, h. 12⅝ in (32 cm)

T'zu Chou ware, which made its first appearance in the Sung Dynasty, is decorated by underglaze painting, a method not in use in Chinese pottery before. The bird designs usually came from Honan and Shantung and were often executed in colour. Here the design is dark brown; the brushstrokes follow the shape of the surface; they have a boldness and freedom, and

convey an impression of swiftness of hand, which bring to mind the drawings of Rembrandt.

The vase belongs to the W. H. Kent collection of Chinese art presented in 1938.

TAI CHIN (active 1430–1450)   Chinese
Landscape with Water Buffalo
Ink on silk, monochrome with slight touches of colour, 67 × 32½ in (170.2 × 82.5 cm)

Below, in the middle distance, a cowherd leads a water buffalo across a bridge; in front of him rise some rocks bearing twisted, gnarled pines, one

of which, half broken, hangs over the valley below; behind them a couple of shrines nestle among the rocks. We shift focus and are transported above the mist into the distance among yet higher peaks. Needless to say the scene is a composite, imaginary one. The motifs used here had become standard themes for landscape painters in the Sung period (A D 960–1279). Tai Chin employs the traditional way of indicating depth by overlapping and by placing small, faraway features higher up on the scroll. By showing the foreground as if seen from a great height, foreground and distance are brought together in scale. There is no logical connection between the upper and lower zones of the landscape. Empty and decorated spaces balance each other in a harmonious design; precise line work alternates with soft washes and the animation of the curving contours echoes the rhythm of nature.

Tai Chin was the founder of an important school of painting, which was based on the masters of the Sung period.

The scroll was acquired in 1952 under the terms of the Felton Bequest.

HOYSALA DYNASTY (12th century)   Indian
Dancer
Stone figure, h. 34¾ in (88.3 cm)

This figure belongs to a sequence of four; the remaining three are in the British Museum. It repeats an old Indian motif of the beautiful woman who brings a tree into fruit by her touch. She stands in a dance pose, one hand raised to the canopy of foliage, which is carved in openwork (*à jour*) with tremendous virtuosity. Figures like these were used as brackets at the tops of pillars in the central halls of the star-shaped temples built in Southern India under the Hoysala Dynasty. The pose is reminiscent of the hip-shot pose of ancient Greek art, but conceived frontally. The curve of the full body, overlaid by the swinging curves of scarves, gives an illusion of movement which is enhanced when all four figures are seen together, when the varying, though related, poses evoke the impression of a stamping, swaying, rhythmically alive group.

Formerly in the collection of the Earl of Dalhousie, it was acquired from him in 1963 under the terms of the Felton Bequest.

HEIAN PERIOD (9th century)   Japanese
Figure of Kan-non
Wood, colouring rubbed off, h. 74 in (188 cm)

Kan-non is the Japanese version of Kuan-yin. While Chinese sculptors had
stressed the feminine nature of this Bodhisattva, Japanese artists of the ninth
century remained much closer to the Indian Gandhara tradition. The figure
is massive and masculine in type; instead of the ornate grace of the seated
Kuan-yin, a haughty, stern, aloof impression is created. The trunk-like
shape of the wood is inscribed with rhythmic rolling lines of folds in flesh
and garment; the scarves cutting across the form remain close to the
surface. The figure lacks the rich ornament, the bejewelled effect of the
Chinese sculptures. But the present impression is too stark; it was originally
painted, and would have stood against an aureole.

It was acquired in 1961 under the terms of the Felton Bequest.

HAGETSU TOSATSU (1516–c. 1585)   Japanese
Painted Twelve-panel Screen, 1575
Silk, signed and dated, h. 68¼ in (173 cm)

The larger of the two illustrations shows the right-hand half of the screen.
A hawk is seen descending to a riverbank; on the left, beside some flowering
shrubs, three herons have barely begun to take notice, despite the startled
birds wheeling overhead announcing the distant danger; the hawk, above
the chrysanthemums in the centre, descends in a sharp diagonal towards a
startled pheasant which shoots out of the picture.

Tosatsu's work is rare. Only one other screen by his hand is known. His
art descends from that of Sesshu and the priest artists who used a modified
Chinese style, reintroducing into Japan a strong current of Yuan and early
Ming painting. However, Chinese elements undergo a change when
adapted from the scroll to the favourite Japanese medium, the folding
screen. Tosatsu's vigorous brush line follows the manner of Sesshu's pupil
Shugetsu.

The screen carries an inscription which reads as follows: 'On the Day of
the Magic Ball, Sixth Month, the Third Year of Tensho, The Year of the
Wild Boar of the Lower Wood, Hagetsu Tosatsu, Product of Osuma and
Sang Yo, Sixty Years of Age, painted this. [Two seals.] Yuge.' Tosatsu was
probably a member of a warrior family of the name of Yuge.

120

The screen, which has been exhibited at the Kyoto Art Gallery and the Osaka Museum of Art, was acquired from Japan under the Felton Bequest in 1958. It has been reproduced in *Kokka* magazine (Jan. 1900).

YÜAN DYNASTY (AD 1260–1368)   Chinese
Fingerbowl, 14th century
Blue and white porcelain, diameter (with spout) 5¾ in (17.2 cm)

The bowl served for ablution at meals. The scroll under its spout is the remnant of a handle, the water being less likely to spill when the full bowl was held under the spout. The distinctive shape is derived from silver bowls such as were found at Hofei, Anhwei Province, not very far from Ching-te-chen, where the first blue and white porcelain was made. On the outside the bowl is decorated with a semi-abstract design of stylized petals, each enclosing a fungus shape and a circle. On the inside the more naturalistic imagery, including a duck and drake swimming among lotus flowers, may symbolize married happiness (see p. 197). A rare early example, the bowl is the outstanding piece of the fine group of blue and white ware in the possession of the Gallery.

Acquired in London in 1963 under the terms of the Felton Bequest.

SUNG DYNASTY (AD 960–1279)   Chinese
Lotus Bowl, probably 13th century
Chün ware, diam. 4½ in (11.4 cm)

With its nine petal flutings, the conical bowl is supported by a small foot. Both within and without are four purple splashes on the lavender-blue glaze, which has turned a pale brown over the ribs and the rim edge, and has left uncovered part of the foot. Tiny bubbles have burst in the thick glaze and gently dapple the sheen of the surface. This is an exquisite example of the superb craftsmanship and impeccable taste of the Sung potters. The shape, almost unique for this ware, is that of the lotus flower, which according to Buddhist lore is a symbol of purity since it 'rises untainted from muddy waters'.

The bowl was successively in the collections O. Burchard, Berlin, and Schoenlicht (?London) before it was acquired by the Felton Bequest in 1956.

ANTIQUITY AND DECORATIVE ART

SUMERIAN (2200–2100 B C)   Mesopotamian
Head of Gudea
Diorite, h. 9½ in (24.1 cm)

Wearing a hat of curly astrakhan wool, Gudea, ruler of Lagash, is represented with a heavy-jowled face with high cheekbones, a square chin and
broad nose, at the top of which the stylized eyebrows meet, effectively
framing the large eyes. Ancient Middle Eastern art did not create realistic
portraits; Gudea's features are formalized. The head is under life size, but
monumental in its compact simplicity. The highly finished surface of the
satin-smooth black stone suggests that the maker possessed an acute sense for
beauty of material, and it is of interest to note that Gudea himself claims, in
his clay cylinder inscriptions, to have been specially active in obtaining fine
stones: 'In the quarries which nobody had entered before, the *en* priest of
Ningirsu made a path, and thus the stones were delivered in large blocks.
Boats loaded with haluna-stone boats loaded with nalu-stone they brought
to Gudea . . . red stone from Meluhha in great amounts.'

The head probably comes from the site of ancient Lagash (modern Tello),
which lies between the Tigris and Euphrates. Before it was sold in London,
it had been part of a private collection of important Middle Eastern anti-
quities. It was acquired from Sotheby's under the terms of the Everard
Studley Miller Bequest in 1966.

CHALCIDIAN (*c.* 550–525 BC)   Greek
The Felton Vase, c. 540 BC
Terracotta with black glaze and added purple, red and white, h. 6¼ in
(15.9 cm)

This is a splendid example of the black-figure style from a provincial
workshop, contemporary with, and not uninfluenced by, Exekias, the great
master of Attic black-figure work. The inscriptions are written in the
alphabet in use at Chalcis in Euboea, but the localization of the fabric is still
a problem. The unusual vessel is a psykter amphora, used for cooling wine;
originally it had an inner container, and cold water could be filled in
between the two container walls through the holes under the two handles.
On both sides of the vase are depictions of episodes from the Trojan War.
The scene on the reverse illustrates combats between Greeks and Trojans
from Homer's *Iliad*. In the centre, full face, dominating the composition, is
Glaucus. Professor Trendall has suggested that the artist is referring to the
occasion when, according to Homer (*Iliad*, xii, 329ff.), Glaucus' enemy
Menestheus shuddered at the mere sight of him. The effectiveness of the
full frontal view is enhanced by a perspective sleight of hand: Glaucus'
purple crest, which should appear in sharp foreshortening, has been shown
from the side, magnificently framing the fierce face of the hero.

The vase was acquired in 1959 under the terms of the Felton Bequest.

ATTIC (6th century BC)   Greek
Black-Figure Amphora (*c.* 540 BC)
Terracotta with designs in black-figure and added white and red paint,
h. 21½ in (53.3 cm)

Classical Greek pottery differs from the wares of the East by its structurally
articulated shapes, and a colour range limited in the main to orange-red and
black. This ovoid amphora is sharply defined into neck, handles, body and
foot. In the panel, neatly inset on the upper part of the body, a row of figures
and horses form a disciplined order between the base line and the row of
lotus and palmette leaves which fill the space above their heads. Details of
anatomy and drapery are rendered by incised lines, and the exposed flesh of
women is shown in added white, with purple-red used as highlight. The
vase has been attributed to the painter of a vase in the British Museum
(BM F174), who was one of the colleagues of Exekias, the greatest of the
black-figure painters.

A wedding procession is depicted: a groomsman, perhaps Dionysus,
follows the chariot with groom and bride, which is accompanied by
maidens carrying on their heads wedding presents in the form of household
goods, waterjugs and (probably) sieves; the horses are led by Hermes,
whose presence, together with that of Dionysus, suggests that this is a more
than ordinary occasion.

The vase was acquired in 1957 under the terms of the Felton Bequest.

THE NICOSTHENES PAINTER (active *c.* 530–500 B C)   Greek
The Felton Cup
Terracotta, diam. 12¾ in (32.4 cm)

In about 530 B C Greek potters began to change from the black-figure to the red-figure style. On the cup here, signed by the Attic potter Pamphaios and attributed to the Nicosthenes Painter (who repeatedly decorated cups signed by Pamphaios and Nicosthenes, and whose activity falls mainly into the last third of the sixth century), the light figures are now reserved in the red of the clay against a dark ground, which in this cup has in part remained a deeper red owing to a fault in the firing. The change has enabled the painter to work with a fine brush rather than a point and to achieve a greater delicacy and flexibility of line.

The exceedingly difficult shape of the underpart of the shallow cup has been most happily filled with figures. From the left comes Hermes urging on Heracles, who, in a similar pose, advances to greet Athena who approaches from the right in a balancing pose. Before them, brilliantly translated into a square shape, lies the giant Alkyoneus, the guardian of the cattle of Geryon, put to sleep by the ministrations of Hypnos, god of sleep. The walking figures are in Egyptian-archaic style, represented with profile head, frontal chest and profile hip and leg, a static device which here has been miraculously infused with natural ease and movement. The repetitive similarity of poses lends a ballet or mime-like quality to the action and rhythm to the design. (Another view, showing Dionysus, is on p. 191.)

The cup was acquired under the terms of the Felton Bequest in 1957.

126

THE ACHILLES PAINTER (active *c.* 450 B C)   Greek
Lekythos
White ground ceramic ware, h. 13 $^{15}/_{16}$ in (35.5 cm)

In contrast to earlier Greek vessels this vase is coated with a chalky white slip upon which the painting is done. The technique was first used in Athens in the late sixth century, but, owing to its fragile nature, remained restricted almost entirely to funerary lekythoi. These vases were intended to be filled with aromatic oil and placed in a tomb, or at a grave monument, or to be used in funerary rites.

The decoration usually consists of scenes from daily life with some reference to the hereafter. On this vase the painter has represented two women, mistress and maid, carrying offerings in preparation for a visit to the grave. The figures are drawn in undiluted black glaze paint, the flesh tones consisting of a more intense, snowy white, which contrasts with the creamier white of the slip. The maid, wearing a peplos, holds a tray with several looped fillets, together with some leafy sprays. Her mistress, more elaborately dressed in a red tunic with long sleeves, and carrying a brownish cloak over her shoulder and arm, holds a perfume flask as an offering. The exquisitely simple outlines of lekythos decorations inspired early drawings and etchings by Picasso.

Acquired 1972 under the terms of the Felton Bequest on the advice of A.D. Trendall.

THE FELTON PAINTER (active *c.* 380–360 BC)   Apulian Greek
Oinochoe with the Contest of Apollo and Marsyas
Pottery, red-figure with added colours, h. 6¾ in (17.1 cm)

Prowess as a flute player had gone to the head of the satyr Marsyas, so that he was challenged to a contest by the lyre-playing Apollo. On this jug Marsyas' manifest dejection shows his realization that he has lost the wager. The comic effect of his misery is enhanced by the knowing wink with which the bald and squint-eyed dwarf addresses the viewer. Apollo, triumphantly walking up to the judge, is depicted on the other side. While, during the classical red-figure period in Greece, no extra colours were added to the design on vases, later decorators began to emulate the free paintings which had developed an infinitely wider range of effects. Among the local styles in use in the Greek colonies in South Italy, the ornate Apulian manner, of which this oinochoe (wine-jug) is a charming example, practised the addition of white yellow and golden brown. The brown hair of Marsyas is decorated with a white garland; his two flutes are indicated in white. The desire for painterly effects, however, does not obscure the draughtsmanship of the figures, whose eloquent and sprightly line work would surely have delighted Thomas Rowlandson.

It was acquired in 1959 under the terms of the Felton Bequest.

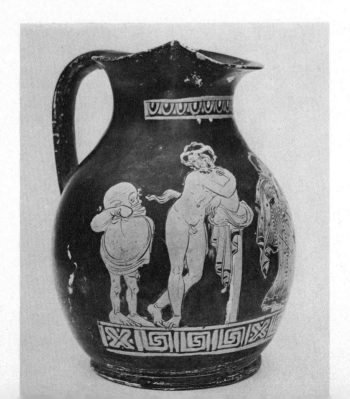

COPTIC (5th to 7th century AD)   Egyptian
Tunic (detail)
Wool, l. 18¹⁄₄ in (46.5 cm), w. 23¹⁄₈ in (58.75 cm)

During the Roman occupation of Egypt, people were not mummified but buried wrapped in the garments they had worn during their lifetime. Many of these garments are tunics, decorated with patterned insets and borders, made from coloured wool. The motifs of the patterns are distinctly Hellenistic, not Egyptian or Christian, but the Hellenistic style has lost its close relation to nature; figures tend to have large heads and rather small legs and feet and are used in a purely ornamental manner. The vine which surrounds them and often encloses birds and animals is also of Hellenistic origin.

This tunic was acquired under the terms of the Felton Bequest in London in 1964.

ISLAMIC (12th century)   Persian
Dish with Dancer and Musicians
Pottery, *lakabi* ware (painted with coloured glazes), diam. 16 in (40.6 cm)

The artists who decorated Greek pottery never aimed beyond two or three colours and had not used coloured glazes. Islamic potters did not continue the Greek tradition, but took up the Egyptian practice of true glassy glazes of colour. In *lakabi* ware, made in Islamic Persia, the Egyptian technique of glazing was applied on fine white pottery, to a carved design which continues the tradition of Persian (Sassanian) themes engraved on open silver dishes.

Three court entertainers appear on a low stage. The dancer in the centre shakes her long sleeves and sets her skirt in a swirl in a dance movement, the rhythm of which pervades the whole design. The drummer on the left sways in accord with his beat, while the harpist on the right is appropriately motionless. The two hyaenas in the foreground appear to join the dance. The dancer's headdress and other details are reminiscent of motifs common on Persian pottery of the Seljuk period.

This plate is the supreme example of *lakabi* ware. It once belonged to the collection of Georges Eumorfopoulos, and was later owned by Tomás Harris, from whom it was acquired under the terms of the Felton Bequest in 1950.

LIMOGES WORKSHOP   French
Reliquary Casket, 1200–50
Wood, mounted with champlevé enamel plaques, 9½ × 8¾ × 4 in
(24.1 × 22.2 × 10.2 cm)

The copper plaques are engraved with figures whose gilt-applied cast
heads stand out against the blue ground strewn with red, light-blue, yellow
and dark-green rosettes. The gabled cover is surmounted by a pierced
keyhole-pattern comb with three finials. On the lid is God the Father,
enthroned and flanked by standing apostles. On the box are two seated
apostles.

The colourful casket is made in the image of a chapel. As its figure
decoration indicates, it symbolizes Heaven, which medieval man envisaged
in terms of the New Jerusalem described in the Book of Revelation: 'And
the building of the wall thereof was of jasper; and the city was pure gold;
the foundations of the wall of the city were adorned with all manner of
precious stones' (Rev. 21:18–19).

Material splendour is a symbol of the glory of God. Reliquaries for public
worship were therefore made of gold and precious stones. Where costly
materials were out of reach, less expensive substitutes achieving similar
effects were employed: the Limoges workshop used a rich enamel technique
previously practised in Byzantium.

The casket was in the Henry Oppenheimer collection in London, from
which it was acquired in 1936 under the terms of the Felton Bequest.

UMBRIAN DERUTA WARE   Italian
Dish, c. 1530
Majolica, diam. 16½ in (41.9 cm)

The decorators of Italian Renaissance pottery came increasingly under the
influence of the painters. The ware made at Deruta, near Perugia, early
reflects the influence of Perugino, particularly in the heads of women which
form one of its characteristic decors. The very shape of the bowl is influ-
enced by the wish to vie with painting: the flat rim carries a pattern
resembling a carved and gilded frame. The bowl is so shallow that it serves
as a circular panel on which the bust is skilfully disposed. Iridescent lustre
pigments emulate the effect of Valencian earthenware, but the motifs are
wholly Italian.

A variant on the profile portrait, popular in the fifteenth and early sixteenth centuries, the head is both fashionable and idealized: the lady wears a sixteenth-century straw cap and necklace, but her tunic, which reveals part of her figure, is surely meant to recall antiquity. Deruta plates carrying profile heads were sometimes inscribed with the names of classical divinities; a plate formerly in the Oppenheimer collection carries the name of Diana, and the figure there combines classical dress with a contemporary Renaissance headdress. The lively drawing, and the bold and anti-naturalistic foiling of the profile with a dark pigment, combine into a most striking design.

The dish was acquired from London in 1970 under the terms of the Felton Bequest.

POST-SASSANIAN (10th century)   Persian
Hunting Scene
Textile, reversible, triple-woven silk in two colours, 17¼ × 31 in (43.8 × 78.7 cm)

Silk weaving was a considerable industry in Persia; many of the motifs of this textile relate to hunting scenes on earlier, Sassanian silks. The palm tree which forms the axis of the composition, the lions and stags, and the costumes of the riders, continue the Sassanian tradition. Earlier hunting scenes, however, show horses in a running position; the rearing horse is closer to Hellenistic usage. The falcons and the stirrups are Arab imports into Persia.

Turnover patterns and circular borders are frequent in medieval silks both from the East and the West. The predilection for these motifs probably arises from the artistic and technical nature of silk weaving, the labour of which is lightened by the reversal of the image. The symmetrical and self-contained unit, continuously repeated over the whole surface of the cloth, forms a pattern of delicate balance and harmony. This is a fragment of a cloth made to wrap round a corpse before burial; many similar ones are extant.

This textile is said to have been discovered in a royal tomb near Teheran, and was acquired in London in 1971.

UMBRIAN SCHOOL   Italian
Diptych with the Nativity and the Crucifixion, c. 1400
Verre églomisé (gold glass) in wooden frame, 8 × 9½ in (20.3 × 24.1 cm), open

The Limoges enamel, previously illustrated, conveys an effect of splendour with non-precious materials. Another such material is the gold glass used here. The procedure was vividly described by Cennini in his *Craftsman's Handbook*: 'wet the glass with egg clear . . . take a piece of gold leaf, of thick dead gold, put it on the wetted glass and press down gently. Put the glass on a black cloth and with a needle bound to a small stick and invoking the name of God, begin drawing lightly . . . the figure you wish to make'. Cennini calls this way of working 'a branch of art in devout use for the adornment of holy reliquaries'.

The diptych here is a reliquary carrying chips of bones of saints, splinters of the Cross and other relics in its frame. It dates from the early Renaissance, but, perhaps because of its holy nature, the decoration is drawn according to the early fourteenth-century medieval conventions which had been in use when the first gold glass objects were made. The artist makes no attempt to render space, the gestures are unemphatic, the motif of the Madonna resting follows Byzantine practice and the fold motifs flow in the linear rhythms of an archaistic Gothic style. The exacting technique may have become known to Italian craftsmen through surviving fragments of late Roman and early Christian gold glass, but it was also in use in Islamic areas. It is now called *verre églomisé* after the French craftsman Glomy, who revived the craft in Paris in the second half of the eighteenth century.

Very similar diptychs are in the Metropolitan Museum, New York, and the Walters Art Gallery in Baltimore.

This diptych was part of the Henry Oppenheimer collection in London, from which it was acquired in 1936 under the terms of the Felton Bequest.

FLORENTINE WARE   Italian
Pharmacy Jar, c. 1450
Majolica, h. 12 in (30.5 cm)

The ovoid vessel is entirely painted in dark blue outlined in manganese purple, with springing hounds amid a close design of coarse Turkey oak leaves. It belongs to the family of *zaffera in rilievo* ware, *zaffera* being the name for cobalt blue (taken from the Persian *al-safra*). Italian majolists owed a great deal to Spanish Moorish potters, whose wares brought the Islamic

135

tradition of ceramics to Italy. The technique and the overall pattern of this pot closely resemble Islamic examples. On the handle, moulded in relief and painted in greenish enamel, is the badge of the hospital of Santa Maria Nuova in Florence, for which this jar was made.

It came to Melbourne in 1936 from the Henry Oppenheimer collection in London, under the terms of the Felton Bequest.

ANONYMOUS MAKER   British
Chalice and Paten, 1535–36
Silver, partly gilt, h. of chalice $4\frac{1}{4}$ in (10.8 cm); diam. of paten $4\frac{3}{16}$ in (10.6 cm)

'But we profess that we must do homage also through the outward ornament of sacred vessels', wrote Abbot Suger of Saint-Denis in the twelfth century. Such homage takes a restrained form in the silver and gold of this chalice and paten, among the last to be made before the reformed

Church of England forbade their use in the Eucharist, ordering the substitution of communion cups. Chalices were first made in the early Middle Ages, and vary little in basic design. Typical of the Gothic style is the clear structural division into cup, stem and foot. The plain cup, gilded inside, is broad at the base. It is supported on a silver hexagonal stem divided by the gilded knop which, with its lozenge-shaped facets and ogival openings, is the vessel's only decoration. The sexfoil silver foot stands on a gilded vertical edge.

The paten, which is both a lid for the cup and holds the consecrated bread at Communion, has a sexfoil depression the spandrels of which are filled with ray ornament; in the centre appears the image of the lamb with banner and cross, and the whole is gilded and surrounded by a geometrically stylized aureole. The engraver has used a design showing the head of the lamb turned back and has rounded its outlines to make it fit harmoniously into the circular shape.

The cup has the London hallmarks of 1535–36 and an unidentified maker's mark of an 'eagle displayed'. It was acquired in London in 1934 under the terms of the Felton Bequest.

ANONYMOUS MAKER   German, possibly Bohemian
Beaker (Reichsadlerhumpen), 1593
Green glass, enamelled, h. 14⅛ in (35.9 cm)

A *Humpen* was originally a welcome glass; the *Reichsadler*, often used for the
decoration of such glasses, is the Imperial double eagle bearing on its wings
the arms with names of a fanciful hierarchy of the Holy Roman Empire; the
design is based on popular prints which can be found as early as 1493. The
decorator employed the Venetian technique of enamelling glass, which was
well suited to the execution of heraldic designs. It is a form of folk art,
striking in the bold effect on green glass of dark enamel, brightened by the
colours of the coat of arms. An almost identical *Humpen*, slightly taller, is in
the British Museum.

   This beaker was presented by Dame Hilda Stevenson in 1968.

Attributed to GEORGE RAVENSCROFT (1618–1681)   British
Ceremonial Goblet, c. 1678
Glass, h. 12⅜ in (31.4 cm)

The picturesque shape, the curving silhouette of which is echoed in the bold

138

linework of the decoration, is in the Baroque taste. Part of the richness of texture is derived from an accident of glass making: Ravenscroft aimed to improve the quality of glass manufacture in Britain, and produced good clear metal with a small lead content. In the transition period between soda glass and lead glass 'crizzling' used to occur, owing to decomposition of the lead, and this clouded the surface of the glass with the fine crackle we see here.

On the lid we read in Roman capitals the words LIBERTATIS ET RELIGIONIS ('of Liberty and Religion'); the bowl is lettered in a cursive hand surrounded by flourishing scrollwork: *Salus Patriae et Ecclesiae* ('Safety of Country and Church').

In the seventeenth century, English-made glass was often exported to Holland to be decorated by diamond-point engravers. This goblet is thought to have been inscribed by the Leiden poet, playwright and cloth-merchant W. J. van Heemskerk (1613–92), who, late in life, started to engrave glasses with verse and proverbs in an elaborate calligraphic manner. The name of Elizabeth Crama, Leiden glass engraver, has also been mentioned.

The goblet was acquired in London in 1968 under the terms of the Felton Bequest.

ANONYMOUS MAKER   British
Two-handled Cup, 1682–83
Silver with repoussé work, h. 4$^1/_{16}$ in (10.3 cm)

The reign of Charles II, during which this cup was made, retained close
connections with Protestant Holland. Dutch craftsmen reached European
pre-eminence in the silversmith's art in the seventeenth century. The finely
embossed 'lobar' style of the van Vianens and of Lutma the Elder gave way,
in the second half of the century, to simpler surfaces chased with flower
tendrils and figures, with which the repoussé work on the bulbous Baroque
body of the cup here has a family resemblance.

On one side the unicorn, a fabulous beast with the body of a horse, the tail
of a lion and a single horn on its forehead, races wildly ahead, while a lion is
similarly engaged on the far side; it is hard to tell who chases whom.
Craftsmen of the Middle Ages had depicted legends of the hunt of the
unicorn and its capture by a virgin. The chase depicted here is related in
Spenser's *Faerie Queene;* it may also remind us of the nursery rhyme
inspired, perhaps, by the British coat of arms:

> The lion and the unicorn
>   Were fighting for the crown;
> The lion beat the unicorn
>   All about the town.

The cup has the London hallmarks for 1682–83, and the maker's mark of a goose in a dotted circle. The early history of the cup is unknown, but the presence of the symbols of royalty may suggest palace origin.

The cup was acquired in London in 1932 under the terms of the Felton Bequest.

MATTHEW BOULTON (1728–1809)   British
JOHN FOTHERGILL (born c. 1700)
The Titus Clock
Ormulu and gilt, h. 18 in. (45.7 cm)

Crowned with the imperial laurel and attired in a toga, the Emperor Titus addresses us with the words engraved on the pedestal, DIEM PERDIDI. These

words are taken from the life of Titus by Suetonius, who wrote that 'Once at table, because during the whole day he had performed no act of generosity to anyone, he exclaimed, "Friends, I have wasted a day!"' Though not without irony as a motto for a clock, the saying is intended to remind us of the transience of life, the conflict between mortality and ethos.

The delicately wrought figure of Titus, so close to classical statues of emperors, and the finely proportioned pedestal and base, enriched with meander and egg-and-dart patterns, acanthus and laurel leaves, and an imperial eagle, testify to the taste for archaeological accuracy, one of whose early English exponents was Sir William Chambers, with whom Matthew Boulton had close contact. Not only the style of the clock but the noble moral sentiment of its theme are characteristic of the Neoclassical age.

The Titus design is said to date from 1772: Boulton and Fothergill repeated it with variations several times. The works of the Melbourne clock are by Benjamin Vuillamy. Originally in the Royal Collections, it was acquired in 1972 under the terms of the Felton Bequest on the advice of Nicholas Goodison and was exhibited at Osterley Park House, London, September–November 1972, as part of the exhibition 'Early Neo-classical Furniture in Britain 1755–1780'.

ANONYMOUS MAKER (18th century)   British
Ceremonial Goblet, c. 1750
Glass, cut and engraved, h. 15⅞ in (40.3 cm)

The transparent linear decoration on the 1678 goblet (p. 139) easily merges into the shape of the glass; the opaque wheel-engraving on this later goblet obstructs its transparency, but the virtuoso engraver has used the brilliant device of composing his design around the interior as well as the exterior of the cup. We seem to look through a decorative arch into the courtyard of the great turreted mansion, which is engraved on the far side of the bowl; the eye is attracted by a small fountain, surrounded by seven Scotch firs, which is located just inside the gate; a bird rises out of the water, water cascading from its beak; in the garden grow daffodils with oak-leaf petals, carnations and other flowers, on which bumblebees and butterflies are about to settle. The rim of the lid is strewn with honeysuckle, daffodils with oak-leaf petals, and thistle leaves.

The goblet is believed to have been commissioned by one of the secret supporters of the Stuart succession and the decorations to contain hidden

allusions to the Jacobite cause. The mansion may be that of the Scottish laird, McDonald Kinloch of Moidart, who housed the Young Pretender after his landing on the Scottish coast in 1745. The fountain perhaps recalls the 'Princes'Well' at Moidart, and the bird is possibly a Jacobite symbol. The young firtrees are believed to allude to the seven young lairds of Moidart who lost their lives after the defeat of the Pretender at Culloden. Many of the flowers are Jacobite symbols.

The goblet came to the Gallery in 1972 from the G. Gordon Russell collection, through the William and Margaret Morgan Endowment.

BOW WARE   British
Henry Woodward and *Kitty Clive*, 1750
Soft paste porcelain figures, white, h. 10$^1/_8$ in (25.7 cm), 10$^3/_4$ in (27.3 cm)

English eighteenth-century porcelain manufactories followed the Meissen manufactories both in technique and subject-matter; individual predilections nevertheless made their mark. Instead of the harlequins, mezzetins and columbines of Italian comedy, used by Meissen modellers, English potters preferred popular local actors from the dramatic stage, of whom engravings were readily available.

Both actors depicted here by the Bow modeller had won success on the London stage in Garrick's farce *Lethe*: Henry Woodward had been painted

by Francis Hayman in the role of Mr Riot, the Fine Gentleman, and the portrait had been engraved in mezzotint by McArdell. Charles Mosley's engraving of Kitty Clive in the role of Mrs Riot, the Fine Lady, was probably based on a drawing by Worlidge once in the collection at Strawberry Hill. Both porcelain figures, however, are carried out with a certain witty overemphasis and light-hearted mockery which is absent from their engraved prototypes, but which is part of the Meissen tradition.

Porcelain figures came to be made in Germany as table decorations, a function often previously served by figures modelled in wax or sugar. The author J. T. Smith saw in 1825 in Garrick's villa a whole group of porcelain figures of English actors, including examples of the ones here, but it is not known what purpose they served.

The pieces came to the Gallery in 1942 as part of the Colin Templeton gift, a collection of predominantly English porcelain.

CHAMPION'S FACTORY, BRISTOL   British
The Seasons: Winter, Autumn, c. 1775
Hard paste porcelain figures, h. 9¾ in (24.7 cm) each

While the Bow figures reproduced on the preceding page still reflect the Rococo style, the Bristol Seasons, made some twenty years later, are decidedly Neoclassicist. Rococo figures of the Seasons, such as the Chelsea

ones, were clad in pastoral costume, often set against elaborate foliage and executed in a mixture of fancy and realism. Neoclassicist taste returned to the ideals of classical antiquity, in costume, in proportions and in plainness of silhouette, and added to these a sweet air of sensibility reminiscent of paintings by Angelica Kauffmann. The classical features of the Seasons here reflect the instructions to his modeller issued by Richard Champion, the Director of the Castle Green factory at Bristol: 'Antique robes are very easy, and have a propriety which is not to be met with in foreign dress.' The modeller to whom he gave these instructions was probably the Frenchman Pierre Stéphan, who was active in England in the second half of the eighteenth century and took his women and children frequently from the paintings of Angelica Kauffmann. The maker (or 'repairer') was Tebo, whose mark occurs on the figures.

The figures came into the possession of the Gallery in 1942 as part of the Colin Templeton gift of predominantly English porcelain.

ROBERT ADAM (1728–1792)   British
Side Table, c. 1780
Carved and gilt wood, 35½ × 48½ × 23½ in (77.6 × 123.2 × 59.6 cm)

Robert Adam, together with William Chambers, was the leading architect
of English Neoclassicism. He excelled in decorative interiors which he
conceived in a new spirit of lightness and intimacy. Standing on fluted legs,
the marble top rests on an apron decorated with a finely carved frieze of urns
in plant-form pedestals. The pierced swag decoration to the apron is backed
with wrought iron to prevent damage. The classical motifs are combined
into a design of great delicacy and rhythmic movement. Drawings by
Robert Adam in Sir John Soane's Museum, London, dated May 1778, are
the source of the design, but these drawings had already been used for tables
for Lady Bathurst of Apsley House and for the Archbishop of York. Most of
the features of the design were already present in a similar combination in
the table which Adam designed in 1771 for the Velvet Dining Room at
Saltarn House.
    Acquired under the terms of the Felton Bequest in 1970.

PAUL STORR (active 1792–1821)   British
Two-handled Cup and Cover, 1806–7
Silver gilt, h. 13¹⁵/₁₆ in (35.4 cm)

'Massiveness is the principal character of good plate . . . good chasing may
be considered a branch of sculpture', wrote C.H. Tatham in 1806 in his
Design for Ornamental Plate, from which Paul Storr borrowed many of his
ideas. The classical kantharos, the loving-cup and the rosewater bowl are the
prototypes of this vessel, which was made as an ornamental showpiece to be
fixed to a plinth. The band of acanthus leaves and floral motifs around the
edge of the cup is a free variant on the decoration of Roman silver vessels of
the third century. The use of heads to mask the handle joints also has a
classical Roman usage. The cut-out and applied acanthus ornament, at the
bottom of the bowl and on the cover, has the strength and fineness of relief
sculpture, while the monumental size and structural clarity of the cup
convey that sense of massiveness demanded by Tatham. The Empire period's Neoclassical taste is well embodied in this vessel.

The cup bears the London Hallmarks for 1806–07 and the maker's mark of Paul Storr, as well as an unidentified coat of arms. It was acquired in London in 1922 under the terms of the Felton Bequest.

ANONYMOUS MAKER (mid 19th century)   New Guinea
Ancestor Figure (Gwalandu)
Wood, painted and carved, h. 102 in (259 cm)

The large head of the *Gwalandu* is surmounted by a cockatoo and four hornbills, and it stands on yet another hornbill. *Gwalandu* means father's father; such figures, believed to house the spirit of an ancestor, are kept in a semi-recumbent position in cult houses, where they are entreated to influence the yam harvest on which much of the livelihood of the Maprik tribe depends. The ancestor figure may also be entreated for the birth of male children. As wood is impermanent in tropical areas, such figures have to be frequently copied; the abstract style will have developed from the desire of the carver to stress the spirit nature, the 'other than natural' character, of the

148

figure, and from the attempt of the copyist to adhere to shapes sanctioned by tradition. The head, seat of the soul of the deceased, has been emphasized; the sharply undercut eyes lend a fierce authority of expression which enhances the protective power of the *Gwalandu*. The decoration, consisting of red and yellow ochre and incisions, indicates the tribe to which the ancestor belongs.

The *Gwalandu* here has a personal name, Charal, but no individual features. It was carved with metal tools, probably some time before 1884, the date of the German annexation of north-eastern New Guinea.

The figure was presented to the Gallery by Mr R. Shelmerdine in 1965.

AUSTRALIAN PAINTING
AND SCULPTURE

Tom Roberts (1856–1931)   Australian
Shearing the Rams, 1889–90
Oil on canvas, 47 × 71 in (119.4 × 180.2 cm)

The leader of the Melbourne Impressionists in the 1880s, Roberts had
basically more affinity with Courbet than with Monet and the French
Impressionists. A realist, he searched for truth among the characteristic
aspects of life. His rendering of country life brought a truly national subject
into Australian art. The scene in the shearing shed is not based merely on a
momentary impression; the artist does not abandon traditional skills for a
'snapshot'. He made his drawings in the shed at Brocklesby station in New
South Wales, but composed and painted his canvas in his studio with
shearers posing for him when needed. Roberts wrote the following expla-
nation of his aims: 'it seemed that [in the woolshed] I had the best expression
of my subject, a subject noble enough and worthy enough, if I could express
the meaning and the spirit of strong masculine labour . . . and the great
human interest of the whole scene. . . . I believe . . . that by making it the

perfect expression of one time and one place, it becomes art for all time and of all places.'

It was acquired in 1932 under the terms of the Felton Bequest.

FREDERIC McCUBBIN (1855–1917)   Australian
Autumn Morning South Yarra, 1916
Oil on canvas, 27¾ × 54½ in (70.5 × 138.4 cm)

A slightly older member of the Melbourne 'Impressionist' group, McCubbin was bound in close friendship to Tom Roberts. Painters whose work he admired were Bastien Le Page, George Clausen and Turner. He knew the French painter's work from reproductions; Clausen's *Ploughman's Breakfast* he could study in the Melbourne Gallery, where it has been since 1905; Turner he learnt to admire during his one journey to England in 1907.

McCubbin's house in the suburb of South Yarra was surrounded by a large garden, to which he repeatedly turned for his subjects. A picturesque wilderness, where beneath unpruned fruit trees and along a leaning wooden fence the chickens peck in the long grass, has been transformed by palette knife and square brush into a pastoral idyll. McCubbin has here reached the style of his old age: a highly wrought surface of marks and flicks of crimson, light green, mellow brown, delicate blue and pink paint, set down with the mastery of life-long practice, creates a trembling veil which evokes rather than describes its subject. The pearly hues of the clouds and the tender transparent blues of the distance are a hymn of praise to the great love of the painter's later years, the works of Turner.

It was purchased in 1955 from C. Traill, who had it from the artist.

WILLIAM FRATER (b. 1890)   Australian
The Red Hat, 1937
Oil on canvas, $36\frac{5}{8} \times 28\frac{7}{8}$ in (93 × 73.4 cm)

The title is taken from the vivid cherry red of the hat which dominates an otherwise near monochrome picture. Frater's understanding of the methods of Cézanne is evident here in the narrow space, the definition of areas by their edges, and the feeling for planes allied to a sense of light. These methods, standing in striking contrast to the tonal realism which prevailed in Melbourne until the 1930s, is one of the early instances of modernist development in Australia. William Frater knew post-Impressionist paintings only from reproductions, but his enthusiasm fired a whole group of young painters.

This work was acquired in 1943 under the terms of the Felton Bequest.

WILLIAM DOBELL (1899–1970)   Australian
My Lady Waits, 1937
Oil on board, 9¼ × 7¼ in (23.4 × 18.5 cm)

While Drysdale made Australians conscious of their country towns, Dobell
was one of the first to look for human scenes in metropolitan areas. During
the 1930s in London he recorded small everyday events: the lady waits,
perhaps, in Mayfair. Observations of this kind recall those made by Daumier or Toulouse-Lautrec, but they are a passing phase in Dobell's *œuvre*.
The almost monochrome treatment, from the deep dark-brown of the
background to the golden brown tones of the figure, increase the fascination
of the red shoes. Dobell's delicate handling of the brush and his sure sense of
tonal affinities reveal a notable talent which was later to find its full
expression in a sequence of distinguished portraits.

It was acquired in 1962 under the terms of the Felton Bequest from the
collection of Norman Schureck.

RUSSELL DRYSDALE (b. 1912)   Australian
Moody's Pub, c. 1941
Oil on panel, 19½ × 23½ in (49.5 × 59.7 cm)

During the 1930s a lively awareness of contemporary art developments abroad grew up in Australia. Russell Drysdale was well acquainted with Cubism, Expressionism, Fauvism and other trends, which he absorbed naturally during his formative period. His work drew attention away from the golden plains and the sheep industry, which had figured so largely in the work of Arthur Streeton and his Impressionist followers, and focused on quite a different aspect of the country: the life of the small outlying country towns, often the reduced remains of former boom period settlements. With the Expressionist's freedom of draughtsmanship, and using colour for impact rather than description, Drysdale has rendered the pub with its cast-iron verandah, the hairdresser, the garage, the vintage car, typical of hundreds of towns of this kind. Hardy country types are wittily lined up, as if posing for an old-fashioned photograph.

   This work was purchased for the Gallery in 1942.

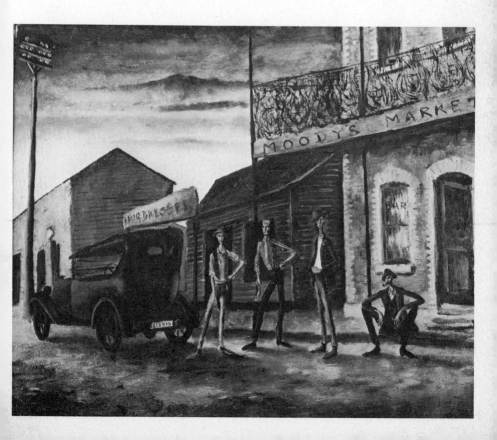

SIDNEY NOLAN (b. 1917)   Australian
Burke and Wills at the Gulf, 1962
Synthetic enamels on hardboard, 48$^{1}/_{16}$ × 59$^{7}/_{8}$ in. (122 × 152 cm)

Nolan is often concerned with events from the Australian past, enacted in the back country. In 1949 and 1950, he flew for the first time over the unending stretches of the pink, dusty, eroded desert interior which turned his thoughts towards the experiences of the early explorers. John O'Hara Burke and William Wills had led an expedition from Cooper's Creek, north of Adelaide, to the Gulf of Carpentaria, and had perished in the desert on the return journey.

In 1952, Nolan began to depict incidents from this expedition, sometimes conveying its fateful nature by the inclusion of huge, symbolic birds. In the painting illustrated, every detail of the scene partakes of the nature of a delirious dream. One naked explorer slides off the rump of an already desiccated camel. The other, disappearing into the distance, is perched, naked, the wrong way round on his mount. The desert swirls like a sea, and the explorers' images are reflected in it. Nolan's deft and delicate handling of paint further accentuates the mirage-like unreality of the scene.

The painting was acquired from the artist by John Reed, who presented in to the Gallery in 1972.

ARTHUR BOYD (b. 1920)   Australian
Shearers Playing for a Bride, 1957
Oil and tempera on board, $59^{1}/_{16} \times 69^{1}/_{8}$ in (150 × 175.6 cm)

This is one of the key works in Arthur Boyd's most discussed series, *Love,
Marriage and Death of a Half Caste*, which was painted between 1957 and
1959, and which raised the artist from a 'rebel and precursor' to a master and
leader. Critics have commented on the inspiration derived from Chagall:
the theme of the bride, the folklore element, the balladic vein, the dream
logic may be compared, and undoubtedly Boyd was aware of Chagall's art,
just as on occasions he has shown his awareness of Picasso. The significance
of the series does not, however, end here. Boyd had been deeply moved by
the degradation of the detribalized aborigines he had seen on a visit to Alice
Springs made in 1951. The bride is part of the Half Caste's dream, which
mirrors his desires and anxieties. In this picture, he appears threefold,
gambling under a lamp (of love, of dream?), the light of which attracts
insects to their death. He tries to retain his dream bride by sitting on the
bridal train. Holding the bridal posy, emblem of erotic fulfilment, the bride
is beset by the ram, Boyd's symbol of the creative element in man. The
insects around the lamp foreshadow the hero's death. The marionette-like
simplicity of the figures owes something to Boyd's pottery sculpture of
the 1950s.

This work was presented by Tristan Buesst in 1958.

CHARLES CONDER (1868–1909)   British
Sketch Portrait, 1889
Oil on board, $5\,^5/_8 \times 3\,^5/_8$ in (14.3 × 9.2 cm)

158

The youthful woman whose red feather hat, above a mere suggestion of face and figure, beckons so enticingly to the viewer, has sometimes been thought to be Miss Janet Achurch, the English actress. Her performance as Norah in Ibsen's *The Doll's House* fascinated the young Charles Conder, who had been sent to Australia to be trained as a surveyor. He stayed from 1884 to 1890. In Melbourne, Conder became a member of the local Impressionists led by Tom Roberts. His orchards and beach scenes, his city streets and country lanes, as well as his few small portraits, have a felicity of placing and delicacy of touch and colour, betraying that decorative talent with which he later made such a notable contribution to the art of the *fin de siècle* in England.

The picture was owned in the 1890s by Theodore Fink and came by descent to Rodney Timmins, from whose estate it was acquired in 1971.

ARTHUR STREETON (1867–1943)   Australian
The Purple Noon's Transparent Might, 1896
Oil on canvas, 48 × 48 in (121.9 × 121.9 cm)

Streeton was one of the young Melbourne painters who, in the late 1880s, formed a 'brotherhood' under the banner of Impressionism. Painting in the open, Streeton captured aspects of the local scenery which differed from English and European nature, and created an image of the Australian countryside which dominated the vision of artists and patrons for several generations.

The Purple Noon is one of a series painted at the Hawkesbury River in New South Wales. In the dryness of summer the water has receded from the river banks; through the grey-green gums the eye travels towards the heat haze of the horizon which veils the Blue Mountains. Low down on the left, cows have come to drink – the only inhabitants of this pastoral paradise.

Set down with great technical aplomb and an almost photographic air of truth, the picture was yet 'completed with a kind of artistic intoxication with thoughts of Shelley in my mind':

> The sun is warm, the sky is clear,
> The waves are dancing fast and bright;
> Blue isles and snowy mountains wear
> The purple noon's transparent might.

It was acquired in 1896 from the artist's exhibition in Melbourne.

LEONARD FRENCH (b. 1928)   Australian
Death in the Garden, 1960
Enamel on hessian-covered hardboard, 80 × 72 in (203 × 182.9 cm)

An unusual example of current dissatisfaction with the tradition of the easel painting is Leonard French's creation – in mural proportions – of enamelled panels which convey the impression of highly wrought, precious objects. Restricting himself to the use of a geometric world of forms, consisting of squares, circles, half-circles, rings and crosses, and incorporating a number of formalized references to vegetation and animal life, he creates an ordered yet dynamic pattern – a pattern which is as rich in meaning as it is sumptuous in effect.

Part of a *Genesis* series, *Death in the Garden* is a meditation on the story of Cain slaying Abel. Indicated by a configuration of circles, Cain stands on the left holding in his outstretched hand, a spear and a shield decorated with seven fishes. The spear transfixes Abel, who lies, in incomplete form, dead

on the lower right. The reversible design of the figures sets up thoughts about relations between life and death, which are continued by the vegetation and the fish and birds in the margin, all of which may connote transformation and resurrection. Acquaintance with the art of Delaunay, Léger and Vasarely, as well as admiration of Celtic crosses and Celtic manuscript illuminations, have contributed to the formation of French's highly original style.

This work was purchased in 1960 from the Helena Rubinstein Travelling Scholarship Art Exhibition.

ARTHUR BOYD (b. 1920)   Australian
Burning Off, 1958
Oil and tempera on board, 36 × 48 in (91.4 × 121.9 cm)

Boyd's work alternates between the two extremes of figure composition
and landscape; these interpenetrate. *Burning Off* was painted in the same
period in which the artist created the *Bride Series*, and the scene has affinity
with the tragic bush settings which appear in some pictures of that series.
Beyond a foreground of undergrowth, gum saplings, heather and dry grass,
the charred stumps, sharply silhouetted against the evening sky or veiled in
rising smoke, glow with consuming heat. As Franz Philipp has pointed out,
'Boyd's Australia is the landscape of his native state, indeed the landscape of
his childhood, youth and early manhood, indelibly imprinted on an inner
vision.... Boyd is emphatically not, like Sidney Nolan, an explorer of
strange lands.'

  Purchased in 1969 from Mr and Mrs Douglas Carnegie, with funds
donated by Mr Roderick Carnegie.

SIDNEY NOLAN (b. 1917)   Australian
Rain Forest, 1957
Polyvinyl acetate on hardboard, $60^1/_8 \times 48^1/_8$ in (152.7×122.2 cm)

Sidney Nolan's scenes from nature, whether in his narrative pictures or in those dealing with the interior of Australia, the Antarctic sea or the forests of tropical Queensland, are almost always hostile or at best indifferent to human life. In *Rain Forest* the peculiar qualities of the medium, which allows thinning and wiping, are exploited in the creation of a dramatic memory image of the dense growth which is foreign and exotic to the southern-born Australian. Though quite precisely evocative of its subject, the picture shares formal qualities with American Abstract Expressionism, which came into prominence in the same decade in which this Australian scene was painted. Nolan made his first visit to the United States in 1957.

The work was purchased in New York in 1959.

FRED WILLIAMS (b. 1927)   Australian
Upwey Landscape, 1965
Oil on canvas, 58 × 72 in (147.3 × 182.9 cm)

At first glance deceptively abstract, the design consists of small formal units

distributed over a flat surface in varying formations, without a centre. The rounded forms evoke with surprising strength the tops of gumtrees of recent growth, which are such a familiar sight near the cities, where the bush has been ravaged by frequent fires. Though the title refers to a densely settled hill district near Melbourne, the artist has avoided all signs of civilization and has recreated a nature uninhabited by man.

The painting was acquired from the artist in 1965 under the terms of the Felton Bequest.

Jon Balsaitis (b. 1948)   Australian
Metron 2, 1971
120 × 156 in (305 × 396 cm)

Perhaps the title refers to the even beat of the surface pattern of short yellow diagonals, which, in an unvarying configuration, are spread over the whole canvas. In the manner of Vasarely's Op art, horizontal, vertical and diagonal forms appear 'behind' the yellow pattern, and may be read as flat or in

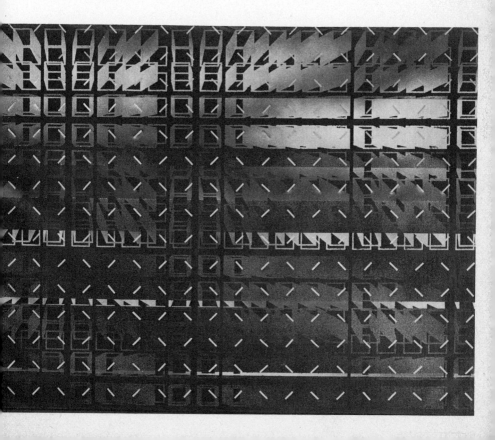

depth. Beyond them a transparent ground, giving the impression of dusky half dark or shimmering half light, seems infinite yet impenetrable. The picture is most meticulously built up from tiny globules of colour which, seen from a distance, combine to neutral tones of brown or grey; seen from nearby, they separate and provide the viewer with an unexpected experience in brilliant hues.

It was acquired in 1972 in Melbourne.

RON ROBERTSON-SWANN (b. 1941)   Australian
Cyclops, 1971
Rusted steel, 48 × 87 × 59 in (121.9 × 221 × 149.9 cm)

The artist, trained in Sydney, later went to the St Martin's School of Art in London, where he worked with Anthony Caro and Phillip King. He returned to Australia in 1968.

Cyclops is a floor-based structure which grows out of the structural properties of its material. Straight shapes are allied to curved ones. The structure is man-sized and invites the spectator to imagine passing through and under. The main forms have basic geometric shapes and combine to a balanced abstract design.

The work was purchased for the Gallery in 1972.

APPENDIX

Additional monochrome illustrations

EUROPEAN AND AMERICAN
PAINTING AND SCULPTURE

School of Antonio Vivarini
The Garden of Love 15th century

Florentine School
Portrait of a Youth c. 1520

169

Perino del Vaga *Holy Family c.* 1539

Prospero Fontana *Holy Family with St Jerome, a Female Martyr and the Infant St John c.* 1550

Peter Paul Rubens
Hercules and Antaeus c. 1625–30

Claude Lorraine *River Landscape with Tiburtine Temple at Tivoli c.* 1636

Jacob Ruisdael *The Watermill c.* 1653

David Teniers II *The Skittle Players*

Thomas Gainsborough *A View at the Mouth of the Thames c.* 1783

Richard Wilson
Llyn Peris and Dolbadarn Castle 1760–63

Joshua Reynolds *Lady Frances Finch* 1781–82

173

Michael Rysbrack *Sir Peter Paul Rubens* 1743

Jean-Antoine Houdon *Voltaire* 1778

Joseph Highmore *Self-portrait c.* 1735–40

George Romney *The Leigh Family* c. 1768

cinthe Rigaud *Monsieur Le Bret and His Son,*
n Le Bret 1697

Alexandre Roslin *Anastasia Troubetskaia,*
Countess of Hesse-Homburg

175

Antonio Begarelli *The Virgin Attended by Three Holy Women* c. 1530

Aimé-Jules Dalou *Sibyll Mary,*
Countess Grosvenor 1874

Dante Gabriel Rossetti *Paolo and Francesca* 1854–61

an Everett Millais *The Rescue* 1855

Arthur Hughes *Fair Rosamond* 1854

Camille Corot *The Bent Tree (Morning)* c. 185

Camille Pissarro *Banks of the Vione, Osny* 1883

Paul Signac *The Gasometers at Clichy* 1886 ►

Walter Sickert *Admiral Duquesne, Dieppe* 1900

Henri Matisse *Reclining Nude*

Balthus *Nude with Cat c.* 1954

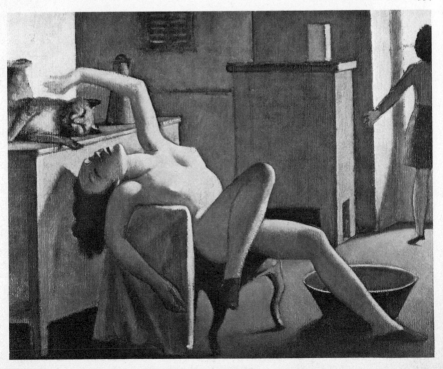

Paul Nash *Landscape of the Summer Solstice* 1943

Graham Sutherland
The Cliff Road 1941

181

Nicolas de Staël *Still-life*

Larry Poons *Cobone* 1970

Gaston Lachaise *Elevation: Torso* 1912–27

DRAWINGS

Andrea del Sarto *Head of a Laughing Boy:*
Sketch for a Head of the Infant St John c. 1521

Giovanni Battista Castiglione *Tobit Burying the Dead*

Francesco Parmigianino *A Stag Hunt with a Huntsman Sounding His Horn in the Foreground*

Carlo Maratta *Jael and Sisera*

John Robert Cozens *The Goatherd. View on the Galleria di Sopra above the Lake of Albano* 1778

John Sell Cotman *Window in the Choir of
the Ancient Church of the Greyfriars* 1807

Richard Parkes Bonington *The Waggon*

Maurice Quentin de Latour *Abbé Pommyer*

186

Jean-François Millet *Spoonfeeding (La becquée)* 1860

Edgar Degas *Woman Drying Herself c.* 1890

William Dobell *Sketch for Boy with Dog c.* 1943

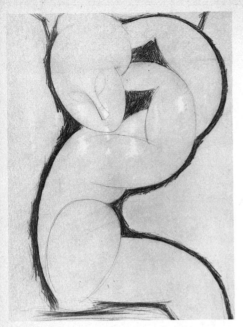

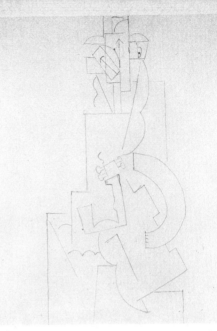

Amedeo Modigliani *Caryatid c.* 1914–15

Pablo Picasso *Man with Guitar* 1912–13

Henry Moore *Study for Sculpture*

ANTIQUITY AND DECORATIVE ART
ASIAN ART

Roman *Head of Septimius Severus* c. AD 200

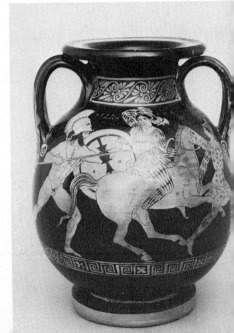

Apulian *Red-figure Pelike* c. 420 BC

190

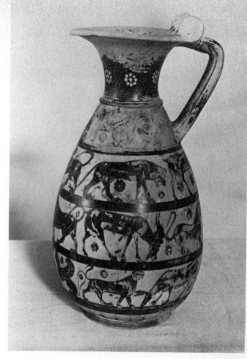

n *Volute Krater* 330–320 BC

Corinthian *Olpe* c. 630–620 BC

The Felton Cup Nicosthenes Painter 6th century BC (see p. 126)

British *Goblet* c. 1760

British *Wineglass* c. 1746

Irish *Rummer* c. 1798

British *Communion Cup and Paten* 1559

British *Standing Salt* c. 1610

British *Toilet Set* 1694–95

French *Dish* Moustiers *c.* 1720

British *Epergne* 1762–63

British *Candlestick:*
Summer and Autumn Chelsea *c.* 1765

Tami Island *Ceremonial Bowl*

French *Vase (with Decoration by Picasso), c.* 1954

195

Warring States Period (480–221 BC)
Mirror with Stylized Bird Design

Shang (1523–1028 BC)
Chia (ritual food vessel)

Han (206 BC – AD 221) *Figure of Horned Animal*

Yüan (1260–1368) *Fingerbowl* (see p. 122)
Ming (1368–1644) *Basin*

Japanese *Mandala* (detail)
early 19th century

Tibetan *Figure of Aryavalokitesvara*
c. 18th century

198

AUSTRALIAN PAINTING
AND SCULPTURE

Frederic McCubbin *Self-portrait*

Tom Roberts *Madame Pfund c.* 1887

Sali Herman *The Lawcourts, Sydney* 1946

Lloyd Rees *Omega Pastoral* 1950

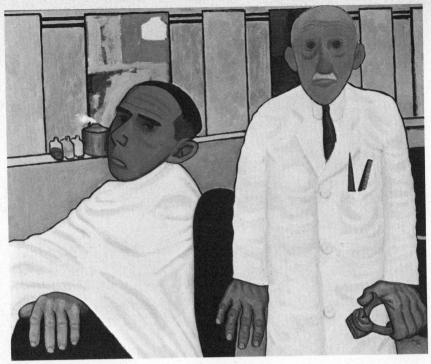

John Brack *The Barber's Shop* 1952

Robert Dickerson *Man Asleep on the Steps c.* 1954

Geoffrey Smart *The Cahill Expressway* 1962

Noel Counihan *The Lobby, Parliament House* 1956

Albert Tucker *Explorer Attacked by Parrots* 1960

Charles Blackman *Dreaming in the Street*

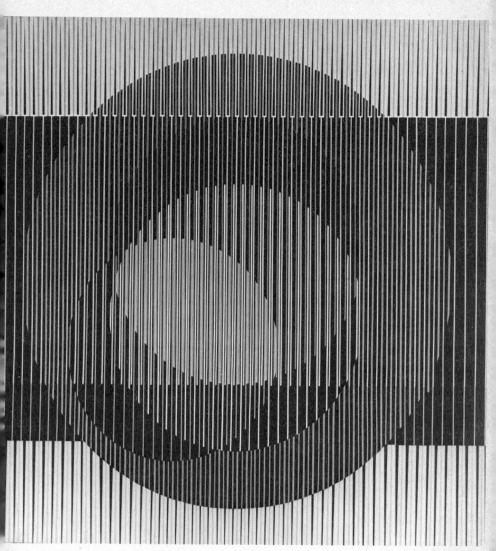

islas Ostoja-Kotkowski *Enclosed Spheres c.* 1965

Norma Redpath *Dawn Sentinel* 1962

Gerald Lewers *Sleeping Bird c.* 1954

Clement Meadmore *Duolith III* 1962

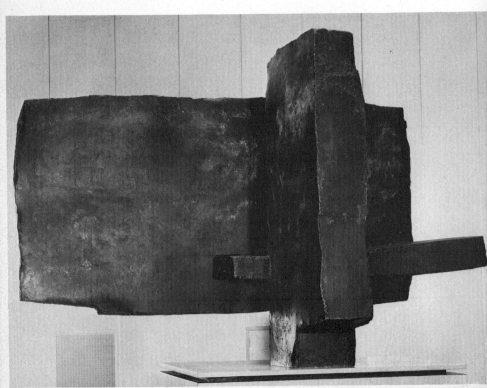

INDEX OF ILLUSTRATIONS

209